# ROCKY VOICES

## The Memories of Minerals That Form the Rocky Mountains

# EVA ENKELMANN

◆ FriesenPress

One Printers Way
Altona, MB R0G 0B0
Canada

www.friesenpress.com

Editors: Janine Young, Ashley Lee

Thank you to the Alberta Writer's Guild for additional developmental feedback on the manuscript.

The author gratefully acknowledges the constructive feedback provided by Victoria Horsman who helped improve each of these stories.

ISBN
978-1-03-916155-9 (Hardcover)
978-1-03-916154-2 (Paperback)
978-1-03-916156-6 (eBook)

*1. Young Adult Nonfiction, Science & Nature, Earth Sciences*

Distributed to the trade by The Ingram Book Company

# DEDICATION

To my parents, who implanted in me the
love for the outdoors and sciences.

And to Brian, who encouraged me to write these stories.

# LAND ACKNOWLEDGEMENT

My stories will take you to fascinating places in the Bow River Valley of the Rocky Mountains, and they will take you hundreds of millions of years back in time. It was only about 10 thousand years ago that people traveled through this beautiful land, which became the traditional territories for the people of the Treaty 7 region in Southern Alberta. They include the Blackfoot Confederacy (comprising the Siksika, Piikani, and Kainai First Nations), the Tsuut'ina First Nation, and the Stoney Nakoda (including the Chiniki, Bearspaw, and Wesley First Nations). Many years later, settlers came to this land, which became home to the Métis Nation of Alberta, Region 3.

# TABLE OF CONTENTS

# Western Canada

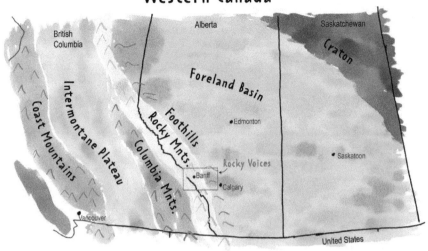

# Rocky Mountains – Bow Valley

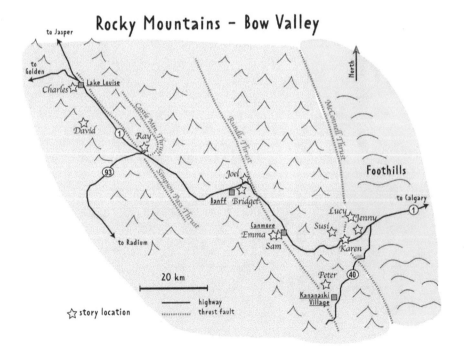

☆ story location

20 km

—— highway
·············· thrust fault

# INTRODUCTION

East — West

old rocks

young rocks

Mt. Rundle Thrust

old rocks

young rocks

Town of Banff

The lofty peaks of the Canadian Rockies are the leftover battle-fields between the west and the rest of Canada. This conflict lasted more than a hundred million years, from the Jurassic through the Paleogene times. And the **rocks** themselves? They each experienced these times of battles in their own way. Each rock is composed of thousands of **mineral** grains. There are many kinds of minerals, each of them with fascinating stories of their million-year-long lives. Most of them experienced the battle that formed the Rocky Mountains, but some are quite young and were born more recently. This book collects some of these stories. Each chapter tells the adventures of a mineral from the time they formed until today, when they all live together in the Rocky Mountains.

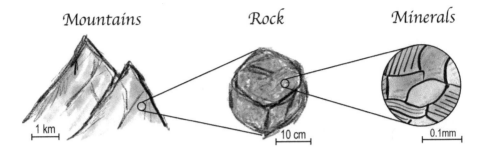

Mountains | Rock | Minerals

1 km | 10 cm | 0.1mm

However, the stories of the minerals go much deeper back in time, long before the Jurassic. The region of western Alberta was a large, ancient ocean that expanded endlessly towards the west. The climate was much warmer: tropical for a long time. Many creatures lived in the ocean, but most of them are extinct today. These creatures formed rocks by building **coral reefs** and dropping their shells and skeletons on the ocean floor. Rivers in the east transported mud and sand from the old **craton** rocks into the ocean. Together, these grains, shells, and skeletons all formed flat-lying layers of **sediment** that covered the ocean floor. Sedimentation went on for more than four hundred million years, amassing 12 kilometers or more that slowly turned into **sedimentary rocks**. But then came the Jurassic times and everything changed. Islands formed far out in the ancient ocean and smashed onto the old craton margin, increasing its size and strength through **magmatism**. These new rocks formed the high Columbia Mountains, found today in eastern British Columbia.

This new western land decided to push eastward. At the same time, the old sturdy eastern rocks of the Canadian craton pushed back towards the west, giving the ocean sediments that lived in between no room to escape. These kilometer-thick layers of old sediment were suddenly trapped in a conflict zone.

The west continued to push forcefully eastward like a gigantic bulldozer. Things got really tight for the old ocean sediments!

That was when the **thrust faults** were born. These large shovel-like surfaces emerged from great depths of the earth heading towards the surface. They first folded the rock that was in their way to later break the rock in front of them. These thrust surfaces also grew sideways, growing to be hundreds of square kilometers. The rock layers above the thrust surface were first carried up, like a big package, and then pushed over on top of their former neighbors. The aim was to grow high and move eastward, getting away from the pushy Columbia Mountains in the west. Over time, more thrusts formed and the same layers of sedimentary rocks that used to rest flat next to each other were now stacked on top of each other, forming a thick pile. This growing stack of sediment layers eventually formed the Rocky Mountains. The thrusting allowed the rocks to survive the squeeze between Western Canada and the east, but it troubled the sediment orders. Most of the rock layers did not lie flat anymore. They dipped shallowly or rose steeply, most towards the west. Some layers were bent and folded. Older sediment used to always be underneath younger sediment, but now rocks hundreds of millions of years older overlay much younger rocks, separated only by a thrust surface. Hundreds of thrusts formed the Rocky Mountains. Some of them moved gigantic slabs of rocky neighborhoods eastward. Superstars like Mr. Rundle Thrust, or his 20-million-year-younger brother Mr. McConnell Thrust (see map figure) moved rocks to the east where the next younger thrusts would emerge.

At the time when all the thrusting was going on, new sediment settled in the shallow sea that formed east of the emerging mountains. This low-lying region was the home of many dinosaurs who were the first to enjoy the mountains. Sediment first came from rivers flowing out of the Columbia Mountains and later from the emerging Rocky Mountains. This way, the mountains of Western Canada grew wider and the sea to the east became narrower. The continuing push and thrust towards the east quickly involved the young river and sea sediments in the battle. They were picked up from underneath by the next younger thrust fault and carried eastward, or sometimes much older ocean sediment rocks were pushed over these younger rocks.

Eventually, the battle ceased. The thrusting stopped just 20 kilometers west of the city of Calgary. The push from the west became less forceful and the mountain-building battle ended in the eastern Rockies and foothills. In the early Eocene time, long after the last dinosaur died, most thrusts officially retired, and the great battle between the west and east ended. The sea disappeared, and rivers started to erode the rocks and shape the mountain peaks and valleys.

Recently, about three million years ago, the climate was much cooler and large glaciers formed in Canada that covered most of the Rocky Mountains. Only the highest peaks stuck out above the endless ice. Glaciers grew and shrank several times, carving large valleys into the landscape. Today, the sediments of the ancient ocean rest on top and lean against each other. Some rocky neighborhoods are folded up and some are hanging in quite awkward positions. That's not always comfy for the rocks, particularly over millions of years. Therefore, adjustments happen from time to time, causing small **earthquakes** you can feel in the area.

Otherwise, all is still in the Rocky Mountains, but the minerals you can find today all tell you about this long history from a different perspective and their own experience. I wrote down the most interesting and adventurous stories experienced by the most important minerals. These minerals are not big, precious, or sparkly. In fact, they are often overlooked in most mineral books. These minerals are important because they compose the many rocks you see today. Have a look at the road map and choose your next adventure to the places of the mineral characters and their stories. I selected locations with the most scenic views in the Rocky Mountains where you can meet these minerals while enjoying a picnic or hiking.

# SCIENCE FACTS

*Coral reef* – An underwater structure built of corals and sponges that form large carbonate structures. They are important places for many life forms and mostly occur in shallow and tropical waters. The first reefs formed 485 million years ago in the Ordovician time.

*Craton* – A very old and stiff portion of the earth's crust. Most of Canada is underlaid by craton rocks. Rocks and minerals of a craton are extremely old— billions of years.

*Earthquakes* – A phenomenon that happens when rocks deep below earth's surface break apart. The breaking shakes the entire crust, which can be felt at the surface in the regions above. Small earthquakes happen all the time and cannot be felt at the surface. However, some earthquakes are extremely large and cause damage. During the mountain-building time of the Rocky Mountains, there were many large earthquakes.

*Fault* – A surface that forms when rocks break into two parts that then move in different ways. Faults can be between a few square meters and hundreds of square kilometers big. There are three types of faults: (1) normal faults form when earth's crust is stretched and rocks slide down from another; (2) thrust faults form when earth's crust is pressed together and rocks slide on top of each other; (3) strike-slip faults form when earth's crust is teared and one side moves in the opposite direction to the other side, causing the rocks to move along each other. Although a fault is a surface, often called a plane, it often appears as a line at the surface that separates the two rock blocks.

*Magmatism* – The process that forms rocks from molten rock, called magma, which forms very deep within earth where temperatures are hot and pressures are high. Molten rock is lighter than solid rock and rises towards the surface. With the rise, the magma cools and becomes a solid magmatic rock just a couple kilometers below surface. Some of the magma rises all the way to the surface where it cools very quickly and forms volcanoes and volcanic rocks.

*Minerals* – The building blocks of rocks. There are more than 8000 different minerals on earth. They are composed of various chemical elements that build specific crystal structures. Minerals vary in their grain size from a few micrometers to millimeters; only sometimes do they grow to centimeter sizes or bigger.

*Rocks* – Hard solid material. Rocks are composed of minerals. Most rocks are a mix of many different minerals. There are many different kinds of rocks based on their chemistry and the way they formed. There are three rock types: magmatic, sedimentary, and metamorphic rocks. Most rocks in the Rocky Mountains are sedimentary rocks.

*Sediment* – Material that forms at earth's surface. This loose rock material accumulates in oceans, lakes, river valleys, or dunes. All rocks exposed on earth's surface break apart and get carried away by water, glaciers, or wind. This material ranges from large boulders, pebbles, sand, and mud to chemicals dissolved in water. After transport, the material settles in the low-lying regions where it forms flat layers that get covered by younger sediment as it settles on top. This process is called sedimentation.

**Sedimentary Rocks** – Rocks formed from sediment. Over millions of years, the sediment is buried by more sediment that settles on top, which presses the grains together and turns it into solid rocks. Most rocks in the Rocky Mountains are sedimentary rocks.

**Thrust** – A large surface that separates two blocks of rocks. On the top are older rocks that were thrust over younger rocks that are below the thrust fault. Thrusting is caused when earth's crust is squeezed together. Most faults in the Rocky Mountains are thrust faults.

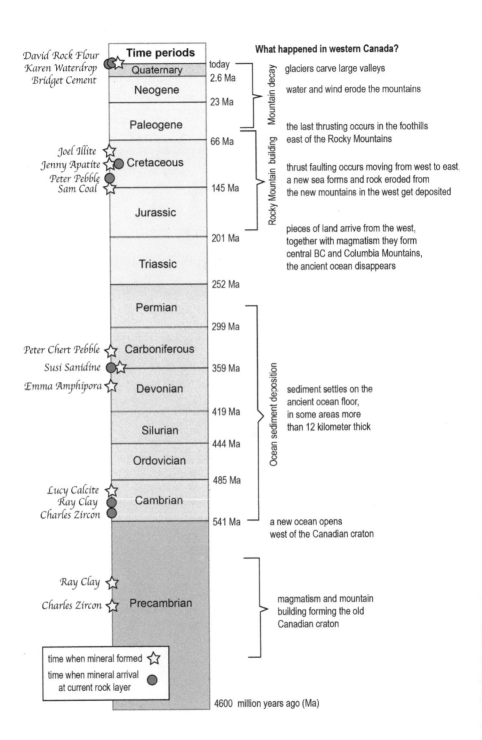

| David Rock Flour<br>Karen Waterdrop<br>Bridget Cement | Time periods | today | | glaciers carve large valleys |
| Quaternary | 2.6 Ma | | water and wind erode the mountains |

# LUCY CALCITE
## Cliff of Mount Yamnuska

Mr. McConnell

Lucy

Location: Mount Yamnuska Parking Area
51.121117°N, 115.086667°W

Scan Me

Relieved from the dark times of burden, Lucy feels finally free as she overlooks the prairies. In the far distance, she can see the high towers of Calgary. The morning at Mount Yamnuska is crisp, but a Chinook wind blows warm air into her face along with the golden rays of the rising sun. "This will be another nice day," she thinks, hoping there will be many more to come. It wasn't always this way.

Lucy remembers where it all started: the cheerful days of swimming in the warm tropical ocean that used to be here. No land in sight. Together with her friends, she would chase the waves and the little critters. Sunlight penetrated deep into the ocean water. This was back in the good old Cambrian days—500 million years or so ago. Who keeps counting all these years? It was long before sharks appeared, and the ocean was filled with the happy giggles of Lucy and her friends. "What a great childhood!" Lucy smiles while recalling those days. However, like for so many of us, these days passed by too quickly. The calm waters eventually made her settle on the ocean floor. Then only occasionally would she go for a little swim. These excursions were triggered by the visit of one of those critters that like to nibble and burrow into the seabed.

"Here, me! Kiss me, kiss me!" Lucy tried to yell as loud as she could, hoping the critters would select her spot and lift her up. She loved those days when she got stirred up again and swirled for a little while through the water. It made her feel young and alive, twirling through the water with her friends before settling back onto the sea floor again.

Lucy smiles as she thinks back to those early days. It seems like a lifetime ago. She is still in her best years, mature, strong, and proudly showing the world her light-gray shine that blushes pink during sunrise, but she has already been through a lot. It was a long journey to get here. A journey with not only happy days.

Back in the Cambrian times, younger generations decided to also settle on the ocean floor–on top of her. It became harder and harder for Lucy to watch the little ocean critters moving around or to feel the gentle waves caressing her. It was rare now that someone came to scoop her up for a little twirling swim. With every year that passed, Lucy felt more trapped, controlled, and pushed into an increasingly rigid environment. Every year became darker and heavier as the burden of carrying the overlying generations increased.

"I don't know how much longer I can bear this heavy burden," Lucy often thought, looking around to see how her neighbors were doing. They seemed to have moved closer towards her. Too close! Invading her personal space. "Are they growing?" Lucy wondered. "Am I growing?" Lucy looked around confused. "Is everything changing?" The beloved ocean water was squeezed out from her neighborhood. Every year felt drier and hotter, making her body achy and brittle.

In fact, she did change. Slowly, she grew a strong regular **mineral crystal** structure. This structure protected her from getting crushed by the kilometer-thick piles of younger material on top of her. Her spirit lifted, she felt really good. Lucy **Calcite** was proud of her new crystal structure. "Simple and practical, a real classic," she thought. But what she liked most about her new structure was her sheen and slightly translucent appearance. "If only someone could see it in this darkness."

Three hundred and eighty million years of being buried and dealing with the same neighbors can be tiring. Lucy heard all the calcite stories out there, and they seemed all the same. But then, 120 million years or so ago, her life took a dramatic turn. There were rumors of a newly forming land mass emerging in the west. Not just the old boring **craton** that bordered the ocean to the east. No, this was supposed to be a new plot of exciting and mountainous land—the Columbia Mountains. She could not see the Columbia Mountains, but she sure could feel them.

"I feel the stress from the west," she said to her neighbors, who seemed to feel it too. "These Cretaceous times are the best," Lucy thought, awaiting more action. And these new circumstances changed her again. The persistent stress from the west caused her structure to form **twins**, making mirror images of herself that allowed for small shifts and changes on her crystal shape without her breaking apart. "One twin at a time," she said carefully while focusing on forming a twin pattern of light and dark stripes across her entire crystal body. That was the fashion of everybody in her calcite family. Those were fun times, but the real excitement was still to come. As the newly formed Columbia Mountains in the west kept moving and pushing towards Lucy, a new sea emerged above her. "More load on top of me?" Lucy complained, disappointed to be pushed, once again, deeper into the earth. The new sea quickly filled with the eroded rocks from the Columbia Mountains. Rivers formed and the land was green, but this was all kilometers above her.

It was still dark for Lucy, until suddenly, she was swiftly lifted upwards hundreds of meters and then pushed 35 kilometers east. The world around her rattled and shook. Quakes shattered the earth around Lucy, breaking the rocks above and below her. Chaos everywhere. Lucy had to hold on tightly to her neighbors. Now was the time to show how strong their community had grown over the dark times. Her neighborhood did not break. Rather, they moved together as a kilometer-thick **carbonate** sheet to find a home in the newly forming Rocky Mountains.

As the world settled below and around Lucy about 50 million years ago, the sea disappeared and exposed the Rocky Mountains to the elements. Wind, rain, and rivers, all wearing and tearing down the rocks from the earth's surface—little by little, one grain at a time. The young and weak rocks disappeared first, then later the stronger and older ones. Valleys formed and slowly exposed the older rocks to the surface.

Eventually came Lucy's big moment: when she saw the sun again after 500 million years! It was a warm, bright day when a large chunk of her neighborhood fell off the Yamnuska cliff, exposing Lucy. The sunlight was so bright.

"Brrrr, it is chilly." Her voice shivered, and she tried to sort out her senses. Slowly, she became comfortable with being at the surface again. "Look at this view!" she thinks now about a view she has now been enjoying for a couple of thousand years. Holding on to the cliff every day, she watches the Bow Valley traffic. She loves the trees, the flowers, and the smells. She had never seen anything like that before. The world did not have trees or birds back in the Cambrian time.

But the most amazing thing is the view straight down the cliff. Lucy can see what happened during the Paleocene earthquake times. At the bottom of her cliff is the legendary Mr. McConnell **Thrust fault**. He lies flat and rests from the hard work of lifting and shifting Lucy's neighborhood. "What a strong force that was." She had never experienced something like that before or after. It was like a roller coaster ride. "There are the youngsters of the Cretaceous." Lucy looks at the rocks below Mr. McConnell thrust. There are the neighborhoods of Bobby **Quartz** and his friend Jenny **Apatite**. They were the guys that had settled on top of her during the Cretaceous, and now they are trapped underneath Lucy and her old friends from the Cambrian generation. "Now they are the ones feeling the heavy load and darkness," Lucy thinks, feeling a bit sorry for them. "The heavy weight came suddenly for them." She quietly wonders how they are doing.

"What's next?" Lucy sometimes wonders. More and more often, she is tired and does not know how long she can hold on to the cliff. "Gravity will get me eventually—again." Most likely, the Bow River will take her on a curling ride, dissolve her nice calcite crystal, and take her to a new ocean to settle again. But whatever comes next, it will be exciting. That's what Lucy is sure of.

# SCIENCE FACTS

*Apatite* – A mineral that is mostly composed of calcium and phosphate: $Ca_5(PO_4)_3(F,Cl,OH)$. It has a hexagonal (six-sided) cylindrical crystal structure and is transparent. Like zircon, apatite is commonly found in many rocks, but in very small amounts.

**Calcite** – A mineral, also called calcite carbonate, with the chemical formula of $CaCO_3$. Calcite dissolves easily in water and precipitates out of it when the environment changes. Most calcite carbonate forms thick sediment layers in ocean basins, particularly when the ocean water is warm and not very deep. Some rocks are composed entirely of calcite minerals and are called carbonates or limestone.

**Carbonate** – A gray rock that is composed mostly of carbonate minerals such as calcite or dolomite. Most of the big cliff-forming rock layers in the Rocky Mountains are carbonates. For example, Cascade Mountain, Castle Mountain, or Mount Yamnuska.

**Craton** – A large landmass of very old rocks, older than one billion years. Most of Canada east of Alberta exposes old craton rocks. In Alberta, the craton rocks are a couple kilometers deep underneath the sedimentary rocks. Cratons can also be found in Australia, Brazil, southern Africa, and Greenland.

**Crystal** – The orderly structure of atoms in a mineral. Depending on the mineral chemistry, atoms can bond very weakly or very strongly to other atoms, which influences the crystal characteristics. Each mineral has a specific crystal structure that is reflected in the crystal appearance. You can use these specific crystal shapes and structures to identify minerals.

**Fault** – A surface that splits a rock and moves one side in a different direction than the other side of the rock. Looking at a rock cliff, a fault usually looks like a line separating the two rock units. Faults can vary in size depending on how much they move and how long they move for.

**Mineral** – The building blocks of rocks. Minerals are composed of various chemical elements that build specific crystal structures. Minerals vary in their grain size from a few micrometers to millimeters, only sometimes growing to centimeter sizes.

**Quartz** – A very common mineral composed of one silicon and four oxygen atoms bonded together: $SiO_4$. Quartz can have many forms and colors, but most quartz grains have no color and appear light gray.

**Thrust** - The most common type of fault in the Rocky Mountains. Old rocks from deep below earth's surface are thrusted on top of younger rocks. This thrusting process occurs when a region is under compression, resulting in stacking up layers.

**Twin** - Minerals can form twins. The process of twinning occurs when a mineral crystal deforms without breaking it structure. Calcite is the most common mineral to form twins at shallow depths because of stress. Scientists study calcite twins under a microscope and derive information about the stresses at the time of deformation.

# SIR CHARLES ZIRCON
Rock cliffs surrounding the back of Lake Louise

Sir Charles

Location: Lake Louise
51.417309°N, 116.218355°W

Scan Me

Annoyed by the buzzing crowd below, Charles is rolling his eyes as he overlooks Lake Louise and the Chateau Hotel. "These crazy modern times are killing me," he thinks. Hanging on a steep rock cliff high above the lake is not his style. It makes him feel highly uncomfortable and dizzy. Sometimes, he finds himself wishing he would fall off the cliff.

Sir Charles did not grow up here. He is from someplace east, Saskatchewan or maybe Manitoba. That is, he is from the **Superior province**. He was born in the warm belly of a large **magma** chamber—a gigantic bubble filled with lava that sits several kilometers below the surface. He was one of the first **minerals** who decided to become solid and **crystallize**. That was back in the Late Archean era. A long time ago. A very long time—more than 2.753 billion years ago. Of course, he does not remember all the details. How could he? But he remembers the magma oozing around his body. And it was hot! As the magma slowly cooled, other minerals decided to crystallize as well, making his surroundings stiffer and stiffer, eventually rock solid.

Most of his neighbors back then were quite ordinary—he thought—even though they were all shiny and fresh, and some even had color. But he was, and still is, rare and extraordinary. Only few of his kind live in the surrounding region. Charles knows he is the most handsome of all. He has a clear **crystal** structure with a slight honey color and a brilliant sparkly appearance. But what he likes most about this look are his sharp edges. Everybody admires him. "The ladies love me," he bragged back in the Archean era, and even today. That's what he is sure of.

He looks around him at the rock cliff today and frowns as he thinks about his current neighbors. "Do I really deserve to be surrounded by all these dull young guys?" he wonders, looking at Bob and his gang. "These boring brown masses of crystal uniformity. They seem to have no style, no edges or shine." He remembers his more interesting, long-gone Archean neighbors.

Sir Charles is a senior member of the elite Forever Club. He will live forever. Clearly a superpower, but also a curse. Who wants to live forever? Nothing can destroy him. Members of the Forever Club are not known for their humor. They are highly respected members of the mineral society and take matters very seriously. They have to. They are the timekeepers of earth's history, counting the years. That's Sir Charles **Zircon**. He tracks every year like a precise Swiss watch, only Charles started counting 2.75364 billion years before Switzerland was invented. The **uranium atoms** that were built into his mineral structure slowly decay to atoms of **lead**. If Charles wants to know how old he is, he just needs to count all the uranium and all the lead atoms in his body. Of course, there are a few other minerals that carry similar atomic clocks in their bodies and could do his job too, but they are not as strong and stable as Charles. So, it is left to Charles and his kind to carry the clock and keep track of earth's time, particularly the very early days. It's a great honor, but also a heavy burden.

As Sir Charles looks over the lake into the forest, he takes a deep breath. "Maybe not everything is bad these days," he thinks. For sure, he likes the trees, the flowers, and the occasional deer that crosses the valley. And even the crazy birds that visit him on the cliff. Although, they are way too loud and fast for him. It takes time for good things to happen. That's one of his strong beliefs.

Back in the Archean, it took a long time for Charles to see daylight for the first time. In fact, he has been on earth's surface only twice in his entire life. When he was born into the magma chamber, he did not know there was a surface. He did not know there was an up and down, north or south, right or left. Everything looked the same. There was just a slight sense of orientation, a gut feeling of gravity. It took hundreds of millions of years for the large rock masses above him to **erode** and take the pressure off his body. He slowly felt lighter. At first, he did not recognize it, but after a while, he was sure something was going on. Suddenly, cracks formed in his neighborhood and water flushed through them. Soon after, he emerged at the surface and saw daylight for the first time.

"Whoa—that is bright! And the air—it stinks!" he screamed, feeling like he was on fire. But he didn't know if it was from the bright light or the smelly gases. It was a nasty, aggressive environment, attacking everything around him. That's when most of his neighbors did not make it. They just broke apart, **weathered** away, or dissolved in water. There were no plants or animals on land. Not even small ones. He hates to admit it, but in comparison to now, the earth's surface was rather boring. Even in the big oceans, there was nothing but some tiny **bacteria** working hard to produce **oxygen** for a better future. But overall, the earth's surface was not a nice place to be back then. Not a place for wimps, that was for sure. Of course, Sir Charles didn't complain. He just sucked it up and went with the flow.

Charles went on a journey that lasted a billion years or so. He does not remember all the nameless places he went. He was transported by rivers. Sometimes he would stay for a while, but never for too long. He didn't feel ready to settle down and be buried and suppressed by others, so he kept traveling, carried around by the water. Eventually, he heard about a new ocean that had formed in the west. Everyone was excited about it, and Charles decided to check it out.

He arrived at the western shore of the North American continent at the beginning of the Paleozoic era, about 550 million years ago. Sitting on the beach in Alberta, he looked over the endless ocean. "Maybe it is time to settle down," he thought. He was not a youngster anymore and the many trips had rounded off some of his sharp edges.

It was here he met Bob **Quartz** and his family for the first time. Together with trillions of these rounded quartz grains, Charles got flushed into the ocean where they decided to settle near the shore. This was a fun place because the ocean was now suddenly filled with life. Charles realized how much the world had changed over his billion years of travel. The air was not stinky anymore. In the water there were now small bugs and worms that burrowed and dug into the sand. You can still see traces of their activity preserved in his neighborhood today. But the fun ocean times did not last for long. So many other grains followed to the newly formed ocean. First came more generations of Bob's extended family that quickly covered Charles's view of the ocean life as they settled on top of him. Later, others came, such as Lucy **Calcite**'s and Ray **Clay**'s families. This process of **sedimentation** went on for 300 million years, piling up more than 10 kilometers on top of Charles. The water was squeezed out of the surroundings. It was hot and the pressure became almost unbearable.

Bob's gang suffered under the high pressure and hot conditions and decided to form stronger bonds. Instead of being glued to each other, they became part of each other. But of course, not with Sir Charles. He wanted nothing to do with this **metamorphism**. "I am a respected member of the Forever Club; I don't need you," he explained to Bob. He knew he would live forever no matter how hot and sweaty it got. "I don't want to become part of them," he thought and muttered, "I am a zircon—Sir Charles Zircon."

Charles looks at Bob who sits next to him today. He smiles kindly. He hates to admit it, but he likes Bob and his family. "They really earned my respect," he thinks. "Their plan worked out. They changed their lifestyle, and all together survived the years of extreme heat, drought, and stress." This metamorphism not only helped them survive back then, but they also came out as extremely strong rocks and Charles profited from their strength.

The first time he benefited from Bob's family was during the Jurassic and Cretaceous times when the Rocky Mountains formed. All the kilometer-thick layers of various rocky neighborhoods were pushed together from the sides. Charles did not recognize it at first since he was protected by Bob's strong family of quartz around him. But things were moving. Large slabs, hundreds of meters thick, one neighborhood after the other, were lifted high up and stacked on top of younger neighborhoods. The weaker rock communities between the strong ones were deeply disturbed and cut by **faults**, but the strong neighborhoods—like Charles and Bob's—remained mostly unharmed.

Charles could feel that the stacking and building of high mountains had brought him up closer to the surface again. He got excited about the possibility of seeing daylight again. "How different will earth's surface look now," he wondered, "after 470 million years?" It took another 80 million years before that happened, but it did. Charles saw the sunlight again. Glaciers helped a lot at the very end. The ice was grinding off the rock, excavating the neighborhoods above him, but not his rock layer. That is not because of his superpowers, that's because of the strong Bobs that withstood the powerful glacier grind. The Bobs are the reason that he still hangs on this cliff here, high above Lake Louise.

Charles takes a deep breath as he enjoys the pretty view he has from up here. "Thanks Bob—I would not be here without your help," Charles awkwardly says to Bob, happy that he has such tough neighbors. "I am not sure if I would have survived the glacial grind without Bob's gang," Charles quietly admits, questioning his superpower for the first time.

# SCIENCE FACTS

*Atoms* – The fundamental building blocks of matter that form chemical elements. Every gas, solid, and liquid is composed of atoms. Atoms are extremely small and bond together to form molecules or crystals.

*Bacteria* – Very small forms of life that often only consistent of one biological cell. Bacteria were the first forms of life on earth. A special kind of bacteria produced oxygen, which eventually changed the environments in the oceans and the air to allow more complex organisms to evolve.

**Calcite** – A mineral, also called calcite carbonate, with the chemical formula of $CaCO_3$. Most calcite carbonate forms thick sediment layers in ocean basins, particularly when the ocean water is warm and not very deep. Some rocks are composed entirely of calcite minerals and are called carbonates or limestone.

**Clay** – A group of minerals built by sheets of silicate layers that are weakly bonded. Very fine-grained soils are also called clays because they contain many clay minerals.

**Crystal** – Minerals form crystals of defined shape and appearance. Mineral crystals grow from magma or other hot liquid mixtures of chemical elements. Atoms bond with each other in a very specific structure called mineral lattice. Some crystals are very shiny and can also grow very large. Those precious crystals, such as diamonds or sapphires, are used for jewelry.

**Crystallize** – The process of forming minerals by bonding together atoms in a specific order. Crystallization happens mostly during cooling.

**Erode** – The process of removing rock from earth's surface is called erosion. There are many forces that cause erosion such as the power of glaciers, rivers, ocean waves, or strong winds.

**Fault** – A surface that splits a rock and moves one side in a different direction than the other side of the rock. Faults can vary in size depending on how much they move and how long they move for.

**Lead** – A chemical element with the symbol Pb. Lead atoms occur in many mineral crystals in very small amounts. Because some lead is formed by the decay of uranium, the amount of lead within a crystal increases over time.

**Magma** – A mixture of liquid rock material, solid mineral crystals, and bubbles of gases. Magma occurs in kilometer-big magma chambers: large bodies of hot and soft rock material located several kilometers below the surface. Minerals are formed and grow in magma chambers due to cooling.

**Metamorphism** – The process of changing rocks and their minerals through heating and pressuring tens of kilometers below earth's surface. Such rocks are called metamorphic rocks. Quartzite is a metamorphic rock.

**Minerals** – The building blocks of rocks. Minerals are composed of various chemical elements that build specific crystal structures.

**Oxygen** – A chemical element with the symbol O. Oxygen is found in many minerals, fluids, and the air. Oxygen is essential for us and most life. At the beginning of earth's history, there was no oxygen in the oceans or the air, and therefore, there was no life.

**Quartz** – A mineral composed of silica oxide $SiO_2$. Quartz is a very common mineral and forms large portions of rocks like granite, sandstones, or quartzite. The cliffs at the back of Lake Louise are quartzite rocks. They are composed almost entirely of quartz that was hardened by high temperatures and pressures when they were buried more than 10 kilometers below earth's surface.

**Sedimentation** – The process of depositing layers of material in low-lying areas such as ocean basins, riverbeds, or lakes. This material is called sediment. Over thousands and millions of years, more and more sediment deposits and buries the older material. Eventually, sediment is turned into rock, called sedimentary rocks.

**Superior province** – A large region of very old rocks that formed in Archean times. The rocks of the Superior province (also called craton) are in Quebec, Ontario, southeast Manitoba, and northern Minnesota.

**Uranium** – A chemical element with the symbol U. Uranium atoms occur in extremely small amounts in mineral crystals such as zircon. The uranium atom is not stable and decays over time into a lead atom.

**Weathered** – The process of breaking down rocks and minerals is called weathering. There are many forms of weathering such as the chemical breaking of atomic bonds in a mineral or the cracking of a rock through the growth of tree roots.

**Zircon** – A mineral with the formula $ZrSiO_4$ that is very hard and durable. Many rocks contain zircon, but only in very small amounts. Zircon is a silicate mineral with zirconium built into the lattice.

# JENNY APATITE
Rock cliffs at the Kananaskis River near Seebe Dam

Location: *Kananaskis River at Seebe Dam*
*51.093417°W, 115.062417°N*

Jenny is eagerly watching the kayakers shooting down the Kananaskis River. Here, the river merges with the calm waters of the Bow River, which is blocked behind the Seebe Dam. Jenny is sitting in a small rock cliff just a meter above the water. This is the best spot to watch the kayakers. "I love to look into their faces," Jenny thinks excitedly while looking at the kayakers who maneuver their last turns. "It looks like so much fun."

Jenny has not always lived here in Seebe. She grew up in the Columbia Mountains just west of the Rockies. Jenny was born 100 million years ago into a big hot **magma** bubble several kilometers below the surface. When the magma cooled, Jenny **Apatite** and her **mineral** friends **crystallized** and together formed a kilometer-sized solid **granite** body. Some of her mineral friends were shiny black, others glittery, white, and pink. Jenny is entirely transparent without any color and has a unique honeycomb shape. Her cylinder-like body has six sides and six edges, giving her a distinct look. For a long time, the granite was her home. Together with her friends, she lived underground. Everyone was close to each other—cheek to cheek—that's how they crystallized. Sometimes it felt a bit tight and constrained. But overall, Jenny enjoyed living in the granite. After all, that was her birthplace, and the other minerals gave her support.

Only a few million years later, everyone around her started to rise and climb. Jenny climbed up too. That's when she found her passion for sports. "This is exhilarating," Jenny thought, feeling the satisfying rise. As they climbed up, the rocks at earth's surface way above her **eroded** and were carried away by wind and water. Slowly, the heavy burden from the overlying rocks was taken off of Jenny and her friends. They all moved towards the surface.

"I am a climber," Jenny yelled when she finally emerged at earth's surface high up on a mountain peak. It was overwhelming: the bright and warm sunlight, the fresh air, the breathtaking views. Jenny was thrilled and overjoyed. "I feel so light." She looked around. "I never thought I could feel this way." Jenny was incredibly happy to experience such a life-changing event together with her mineral friends. They had reached the highest mountain peak.

When Jenny climbed up to the surface back in the Cretaceous time, she was surprised at how the world looked. Nobody had prepared her for this. She had never heard of earth's surface before. Nobody in the granite rock had been there before. It just happened to her. Jenny and her friends all felt a bit uncomfortable at first, but quickly got used to the surface. After a couple years of enjoying the views, Jenny wondered what would come next. She was a climber, but there was nothing higher to climb. She was at the peak. Somehow, though, she knew that whatever came next could only go downhill.

The changing conditions from day to night, from summer to winter, were wearing on the granite neighborhood. Some of Jenny's mineral friends started to look old. They were not as shimmery as they used to be. Some of them cracked and even started to fall apart. Jenny was worried. Worried for her friends, but also for herself. "What is going on? Am I changing too?" she wondered. No—her crystal structure was intact, and her body was still in its perfect, six-sided shape, but she was sad to see her friends suffering. Even worse, over the next couple hundred years on the mountain peaks, she slowly recognized that some of her mineral friends were going missing. They just disappeared! "Where to?" Jenny often pondered, slightly afraid. "Will I disappear next?"

It was a beautiful day in the Columbia Mountains about 80 million years ago when the summer heat became unbearable and dark roaring clouds formed around Jenny. A big storm came. Large raindrops pounded down on Jenny and her mineral friends of the granite. She tried to hold on to her neighbors for support, but too many of the grains around her were already gone, **weathered** and eroded away. Now, it was her turn. A big raindrop hit her hard on the side. Jenny popped right out of the granite. She rolled on one of her crystal sides. She realized that for the first time in her life, she was not attached to another mineral. "I am free!" Jenny shouted over the thunderstorm. "But also alone," she quickly realized. "Where are my friends?" She looked anxiously around, wondering if there was anyone from her neighborhood nearby.

But there was no time to be sad. The journey began and Jenny the climber became Jenny the river girl. At first, it was only a couple big raindrops chasing her down the mountain peak. Later, it was like Jenny was sitting on a giant water slide. The mountain slope was steep, and she rolled and jumped, picking up more and more speed. "Oh boy—this is fun," Jenny thought as she was flushed into a creek, "but I am getting dizzy. This is too faaaast!" There was so much water! Rushing quickly, the pace was breathtaking. It had taken her 20 million years to climb to the peak of the mountain and it took only hours to travel a few kilometers downhill.

Jenny loved the water from day one. It made her feel alive, mobile, and lightweight. She met new minerals along the river journey. Jenny became an expert in flowing down the river, moving from one side to the other, always following the fastest and deepest paths of the stream. Sometimes she would have to take a break on a sandy gravel bank next to the river, catching her breath. She would make new friends and chat a while, waiting for the next rainstorm to take her on the next ride. That's how she met her new **quartz** friend Bobby Quartz and his family. They traveled together further down the river. From a small creek to a bigger creek, from a small river to a bigger river. Over the next couple years, she got to know a lot of interesting places as she traveled east. Eventually, the mountains around her became smaller and the valleys wider. More and more trees showed up. "This must be the **foreland** in Alberta," Jenny thought. She had heard about this region before.

This was when Jenny decided it was time to settle down. She was a bit tired, and the bumpy travel had taken a toll on her body. Her distinct six-sided crystal was now rounded, she'd lost her edges, and she now looked very much like Bobby or any of the other round quartz grains. Jenny didn't mind her changed look. In fact, looking more like all the other quartz grains was good. She felt more accepted. "I don't want to stick out," Jenny thought. "I would much rather be treated like one of them." Deep inside, Jenny hoped she could be part of the quartz family and that they could all live together.

It was a good time to take a break. The river was moving slowly, and dinosaurs walked around on the shore. Everything was lush and green. "Really interesting and exciting new stuff to see here! This is a good place to be," Jenny decided. "I can still see the mountains and I am close to the river." Bobby and his quartz family agreed, and they all decided to settle. This is how they began to build a new neighborhood together. More and more mineral grains flushed out of the mountains and quickly buried Jenny and the quartz grains. Even some tree leaves, branches, and pieces of wood got buried and mixed into their neighborhood. Over time, these new generations of mineral grains blocked the sunlight and increased the load on Jenny's body.

Jenny felt happy to take a rest from all the exciting, exhausting travels. "This feels nice and cozy again," she thought, cheek to cheek with Bobby and her other new friends. The water squeezed out from their neighborhood and with the increasing pile of grains above her, it became warmer and warmer. Jenny and the other grains were slowly glued together and eventually formed a solid **sandstone** layer. The trapped plant pieces, however, could not stand the heat. They turned dark brown and started to cook. They smelled terrible! It was like having little outhouses distributed in Jenny's neighborhood. Overall, Jenny enjoyed the support of her new family. Sometimes, however, she wondered if she would ever see the river again.

Millions of years passed when suddenly, the entire neighborhood shook. Something big and heavy moved over Jenny's sandstone layer. She could not see anything, but suddenly, the weight on her neighborhood increased to ten times or more. "What is happening?" she asked, concerned. Shortly after, a big rumble started underneath her. Someone was lifting and moving her neighborhood. **Earthquakes** shattered all around. Neighborhoods were breaking apart and bending. This all lasted until the Eocene time, about 50 million years or so. Suddenly, it was quiet. Her neighborhood was slightly tilted, but otherwise intact. Everybody was wondering what would happen next. Would the heavy load on top of them be taken off at some point? This extra load caused even more heat—and the plant pieces stunk even more. "Will I climb again," Jenny wondered hopefully, "up to the surface?"

After tens of millions of years, the load above Jenny slowly lifted. She felt lighter and lighter. "I am climbing again," Jenny realized. Now she was certain they would reach the surface again. She emerged onto the surface in a river valley. She was so grateful to the Kananaskis River, which carved a path right next to Jenny. "Lucky me." She smiled. Jenny was surprised by how different the world looked. There were suddenly mountains around her! The Rocky Mountains had moved towards her new home. "The trees look so different now, and what happened to the dinosaurs?" she wondered. They were replaced by other creatures she had never seen before.

Today, Jenny looks up to the trees on the other side of the Kananaskis River. She is trying to find out how windy it is. When the winds get strong enough, they form large waves and sometimes the water splashes up to Jenny. Right in her face. She loves this refreshing shower. It does not look like it will happen today though. The trees stand still, just a gentle wave of some branches. "Well—maybe tomorrow then."

Jenny looks north, towards the cliff that forms Mount Yamnuska. "This **limestone** neighborhood of Lucy **Calcite** is much older than our sandstone layer, and much older than me, but it is above me!" Jenny is puzzled. Then she recognizes the meter-thick horizontal layer that separates the limestone cliff from the sandstone underneath. She slowly realizes what happened back in the Eocene. It was Mr. McConnell **Thrust** who shoved a kilometer-thick layer of Cambrian limestone on top of her. "That's what made the rumbling earthquakes and heavy burden," she explains to her quartz friends. Jenny realizes there must be more to this puzzle. "Mr. McConnell is above us. He moved and tilted the old limestones, but he cannot be the one who moved and tilted our neighborhood!" Jenny gets excited. Suddenly, she knows there must be another thrust **fault** underneath her, which pushed her to the east and caused the tilting.

Jenny looks at the river. The next kayakers are nearing her rock face. "I really am a lucky apatite," she thinks. "I have the best of everything now." She is at the surface with her sandstone family, and she is near the river. But she is wiser now. Jenny knows it is all a cycle of loss and gain. Soon, the day will come when she will get knocked off the rock face and fall right into the Kananaskis River. She will travel exciting new routes. "It will be sad," Jenny thinks, "but I know there will be new friends waiting out there and we will form a new rock community." Until then, she enjoys watching others having fun at the river.

# SCIENCE FACTS

*Apatite* – A mineral that is mostly composed of calcium and phosphate: $Ca_5(PO_4)_3(F,Cl,OH)$. It has a hexagonal (six-sided) cylindrical crystal structure and is transparent. Like zircon, apatite is commonly found in many rocks, but in very small amounts.

*Calcite* – A mineral, also called calcium carbonate $CaCO_3$, that forms limestone rocks.

*Crystallized* – The process of forming minerals by bonding together atoms in a specific order is called crystallization. Crystallization happens mostly during cooling of magma.

*Eroded* – The process of removing rock from earth surface is called erosion. There are many forces that cause erosion such as by the power of glaciers, rivers, ocean waves, or strong winds.

*Earthquake* – Occurs when rocks deep below the surface break. During Rocky Mountain building, the rock layers were pushed together from the side, which caused breaking of rock layers, forming large faults. The process repeats many times, causing the faults to grow bigger. The breaking process itself creates an intense shaking of the rocks deep below earth's surface. This shaking is what we call an earthquake.

*Fault* – A surface that splits a rock and moves one side in a different direction than the other side of the rock. Looking at a rock cliff, a fault usually looks like a line separating the two rock units. Faults can vary in size depending on how much they move and how long they move for.

*Foreland* – The region in front of the mountains where the sediment that is eroded from the mountains is transported and deposited. Over millions of years, the mountains grow bigger and wider, and the foreland is built into the mountains. At the same time, new foreland forms in front of the mountains.

*Granite* – A magmatic rock type that forms when hot magma cools and becomes solid several kilometers deep below earth's surface. You can find granitic rocks west of the Rocky Mountains.

*Limestone* – A sedimentary rock composed mostly of calcite minerals ($CaCO_3$). Limestone is also called carbonate rock. Most of the big cliff-forming peaks in the Rocky Mountains are made of limestone.

*Magma* – Very hot, molten rock that comes from tens of kilometers below earth's surface. Magma is a mixture of fluid, gas, and solids like mineral crystals and pieces of rock. When magma cools, it crystallizes in many minerals and becomes a magmatic rock.

**Mineral** – The building blocks of rocks. Minerals are composed of various chemical elements that build specific crystal structures. Minerals vary in their grain size from a few micrometers to millimeters; only sometimes do they grow to centimeter sizes.

**Quartz** – A very common mineral composed of one silicon and four oxygen atoms bonded together: $SiO_4$. Quartz can have many forms and colors, but most quartz grains have no color and appear light gray. Sand and sandstone are mostly composed of quartz grains that were rounded due to transport by rivers or wind.

**Sandstone** – A sedimentary rock composed of various mineral grains, often quartz. Sandstone is formed by sand grains deposited by rivers or in oceans or sand dunes which get buried deep to transform into a solid rock.

**Thrust** – One of the three types of faults and the most common type you can see in the Rocky Mountains. Old rocks from deep below are thrusted on top of younger rocks at shallower depths. This process occurs when a region is under compression from the sides, resulting in stacking up layers.

**Weathered** – The process of breaking down rocks and minerals is called weathering. There are many forms of weathering such as the chemical breaking of atomic bonds in a mineral or the cracking of a rock through the growth of tree roots.

# JOEL ILLITE
The Rundle Thrust below Cascade Mountain

Joel and
Mr Rundle Thrust

**Location:** *Cascade Pond Picnic Area*
*51.210387°N, 115.533059°W*

Joel sits just below the rock cliff of Cascade Mountain covered by soil in the forest. He wakes up and stretches his body, bending and flexing all his **crystal** layers. "That feels good," he thinks. "I am getting all achy in this dry weather." The westward-dipping rock layers on Cascade Mountain—that's his work. He and his family helped make this happen. He loves his crowning achievement, those beautiful tilting layers. "It looks so stylish and sophisticated," he thinks proudly. Follow the line of rock layers bending up and down, dipping steeper and steeper. That's what Joel contributed to the world. He and Mr. Rundle **Thrust fault**. Mr. Rundle Thrust emerges at the surface here, just below the Cascade rock cliff, where the trees start to grow on the gentler slopes. He is very long and wide, stretching more than 400 kilometers north and south. Turn around! See the forested slopes below the steep cliffs of Mount Rundle? That's also him. And Joel? He lives right here with him. "I am part of him," he thinks, smiling gently.

Joel is very small, quirky, and soft. He is easily overlooked as pale powder. That doesn't bother Joel. He knows that some find him attractive, and even mysterious, because of his cool **mineral** structure, not his look. He doesn't care much about that though. In fact, he prefers to be in the background. Under the trees and soils that protect him, he quietly supports the legendary Mr. Rundle. And Mr. Rundle appreciates him. Joel knows that a big fault like Mr. Rundle could not have created this beautiful long mountain ridge without any help. For that reason, Mr. Rundle created Joel.

When Mr. Rundle Thrust formed about 72 million years ago, coming up from the depths, he split the rocks deep below the surface, taking the top part off and moving it up and east. Like all thrusts, he is smart and decided to split the rock layer that is the weakest, the **shale** rocks. It's just easier to move within the flimsy shale rocks instead of the tough **carbonates** or **quartzite** neighborhoods of Lucy **Calcite** or Charles **Zircon**. So, he broke the rocky layers and went on, recognizing that it became easier as he broke more rock apart. That is how Mr. Rundle grew quickly bigger and bigger into a large and expanding surface. Occasionally, he would have to rest, running out of steam because he carried kilometers of thick rock layers on his back, aiming to push them eastwards. He built up his strength and planned his next thrust step until he had enough energy to move on. Sometimes, it took him a couple years and sometimes thousands of years before moving again, but eventually, he would repeat the split-and-go work. When the load on his back became too heavy to push it further east, he decided to journey up, towards the surface. That was not easy because of the much harder rocks that surrounded the shale layers. After a long rest, he gathered all his strength and suddenly broke through the thick and tough carbonate layers above. It was a thunderous, forceful process creating repeated **earthquakes** that echoed widely. His motion crumpled up the rocks nearby. What formed was a meter-thick layer full of rock crumbs and newly formed **clay** minerals like Joel **Illite**. A **fault zone** formed. The Rundle fault zone.

Joel was born during these stressful and hectic times in the fault zone where water and many elements flowed around the broken rock crumbs. Lots of other clay minerals were born at the same time, all by forming thin layers of silica and oxide as their foundation. The moment Joel was born, he had to make tough decisions. "What other elements should I take?" Joel wondered desperately. Everybody was running and rushing around him. "I need to make a decision, a good one, and quickly," he mumbled to himself. At the same time, the rocks above and below him moved, rumbling and shattering the earth. "Boy—this is stressful," he cried. "Let's take oxygen and hydrogen to form water. I love water." Looking around, he tried to figure out what elements were still available. Everybody tried to get some good elements to finish building a nice mineral. Joel grabbed what he could get—iron, aluminum, magnesium, potassium. "I will figure out how to put this all together with my silicate oxide layers later," he thought. "I can be creative." So, he started to place some of the elements between the thin silicate sheets that were very loosely stacked on top of each other, always in between a layer of water. He looked like a paperback book with many pages. This design allowed him to store the water and the other elements between the pages, which made him feel more flexible. "This feels nice and bendable," he said when he was done forming. A real crystal, but not as stiff as most of the other minerals. "I need to be small and flexible if I want to live with the energetic and persuasive Mr. Rundle," he thought.

Joel admires Mr. Rundle. After all, he provided the flushing elemental cocktail that allowed him to form. At the same time, he continued to carry rocks to the east. That is why Joel is so small; all that sliding and moving going on during his birth and the following years gave him no time to grow bigger. "Maybe that was his plan," Joel thought. "My small size makes it easier for me to roll along as he splits and goes." He was right. Being small and flexible served him well in a fault zone. Other minerals suffered and disappeared under the rolling load. But the clays survived and thrived.

Joel was happy—if there was enough water in the fault zone. Every time new water flushed into the fault zone, Joel refreshed and expanded his sheet layers. Those were the times when the clay families worked like a jack, lifting the heavy rock load on top of Mr. Rundle. That is how he helped him do his work. Joel and his family lifted the load up and over, one move at a time, lifting and shifting the rocky, kilometer-thick load above the rocks below them.

This is what made Joel's life so interesting. He didn't have to travel far to see new, exciting things. He saw a lot of the mineral world while living in the fault zone. For example, above him and Mr. Rundle are Devonian carbonates Joel knows for a long time. They formed long before Joel's time, about 370 million years ago. But below him today are much younger rocks. The rocks below the thrust used to be Devonian too, but as Mr. Rundle started to climb up, breaking through the rock layers, the rocks below him became younger and younger. That was the only way Joel knew they were going upwards. Today, Joel is sitting on top of **sediment** layers that were deposited 155 million years ago in the sea that formed along the eastern side of the mountains. "We carried the ancient Devonian carbonates over the dinosaur footprints from the Jurassic period," Joel thinks. He is still proud of his work, even though this was a long time ago.

Mr. Rundle is sleeping today. The entire fault zone community has been resting for the last 70 million years or so. He is still exhausted from the heavy lifting and thrusting he did during the days of mountain building, while Joel is getting a bit bored. There has been nothing going on for a long time. Especially compared to the times he was born into—the peak performance days of Mr. Rundle in the Late Cretaceous time.

Joel knows exactly the day when he was created. He has a small atomic clock built into his crystal, similar to Sir Charles Zircon. Unlike Charles though, he counts the potassium atoms he built into his lattice which started to decay to argon gas over time. Yes—it is a bit tricky to count the wobbling argon gas atoms in his body, but he just finished it! That is how he knows he has been with Mr. Rundle for 73.125649 million years.

What will be next? The times of heavy lifting are seemingly over. He is almost at the surface. "Should I go and see the day-light?" he sometimes wonders. It would be fun and something new, but he has heard terrible stories from up there. It is said the fun is short lived: you easily get washed away after only a couple weeks or years. He would dissolve and his elements would feed the forest trees or flush away into the river. "Maybe it's better to stay here, protected by the soil and the trees," Joel thinks while looking around. "He may need my help." Maybe one day the battle between the mountains in the west and the rest of Canada will renew. If one side begins to push again and the other won't give in, the forces may become large enough to wake up Mr. Rundle Thrust and the other fault legends. And Joel? "I will be there to help thrusting."

# SCIENCE FACTS

**Calcite** – A mineral, also called calcite carbonate, with the chemical formula of $CaCO_3$.

**Carbonate** – A rock type composed of carbonate minerals such as calcite or dolomite. Most of the big cliff-forming rock layers in the Rocky Mountains are carbonates. For example, Cascade Mountain, Castle Mountain, or Mount Yamnuska.

**Clay** – A group of minerals built by sheets of silicate layers that are weakly bonded. Illite is one of the many clay minerals. Very fine-grained soils are also called clays because they contain many clay minerals.

**Crystal** – The orderly structure of atoms that determines a mineral. Depending on the chemistry, atoms form strong bonds building a regular crystal structure. Each mineral has a specific crystal structure that is reflected in the crystal appearance. Clay minerals have a typical crystal structure that comprises layers.

**Earthquake** – Occurs when rocks deep below the surface break. The breaking process creates an intense shaking of the rocks deep below earth's surface. This shaking is what we call an earthquake. Large earthquakes can shake the ground and cause damage at earth's surface.

**Fault zone** – The zones around the fault surface where the rocks are broken and deformed due to the rock motion. Large faults such as Rundle and McConnell have a fault zone that is several meters thick. The broken rocks in a fault zone allow water to move through and new minerals to form during the faulting processes. Illite is one of those typical fault zone minerals.

**Illite** – A mineral that belongs to the group of clay minerals. It is composed of layers of silica with water and other elements loosely located between the layers. Because of the layered structure, these minerals are also called phyllosilicate. The chemical formula of illite is quite long and shows that various atoms can be built in between the layers and exchanged easily: $(K,H_3O)(Al,Mg,Fe)_2(Si,Al)_4O_{10}[(OH)_2,(H_2O)]$.

**Mineral** – The building blocks of rocks. Minerals are composed of various chemical elements that build specific crystal structures. Minerals vary in their grain size from a few micrometers to millimeters; only sometimes do they grow to centimeter sizes.

**Quartzite**– A rock type that is mostly composed of quartz grains that were deposited as sediment and later buried many kilometers deep. The heat and pressure turn the sediment into very hard rocks.

**Shale** – A sedimentary rock type that is very weak and soft. Shale is fine mud that settles on the bottom of the ocean or deep lakes. Shale comprises many clay minerals.

**Sediment** – Material that forms at earth's surface. This loose rock material accumulates in oceans, lakes, river valleys, or dunes. This material ranges from large boulders, pebbles, sand, and mud to chemicals dissolved in water.

**Thrust** – One of the three types of faults and the most common type you can see in the Rocky Mountains. Old rocks from deep below are thrusted on top of younger rocks at shallower depths. This process occurs when a region is under compression from the sides, resulting in stacking up layers.

**Zircon** – A mineral with the formula $ZrSiO_4$ that is very hard and durable. Many rocks contain zircon, but only in very small amounts. Zircon is a silicate mineral with zirconium built into the lattice.

# CAPTAIN SUSI SANIDINE
Black shale layer at Jura Creek

*Susi*

Location: End of the upper canyon
of Jura Creek

51.090860°N, 115.159232°W

Scan Me

Here at the upper canyon of Jura Creek, Susi looks at the dark-colored rocks above and below. "That's all that's left of us," she thinks, slightly annoyed. "A layer trapped between black **shale**." She and her gang form a centimeter-thick layer of pale yellow malleable mineral slush called **tuff**. They have been trapped in the shale for a very long time. Susi, though, had one of the most exclusive and adventurous upbringings one can imagine. This was long ago, but she still likes to share her story.

It was about 359 million years ago when the Devonian period was just ending and the Carboniferous time was starting. Like many minerals, Susi formed in a large **magma** chamber several kilometers below earth's surface. She **crystallized** when the magma was still very hot. Unlike most other minerals that crystallized, Susi **Sanidine** did not descend but stayed up high. Here, the magma chamber was filled with a mix of gases, fluids, and magma. The gases wanted to rise higher, but the magma did not. Susi liked the idea of the gases and tried to convince the rest of the magma to rise. Susi and her bubbly gang had a goal—to get to the surface. Fast! All the way up. Not just below the surface, like many minerals. No—Susi and her adventurous gang wanted more. She felt she was made for bigger things than crystallizing deep underground; she wanted to be a pilot, rocketing all the way up to the sky.

Her determination and hard work to convince the others in the magma chamber paid off. When the pressures at the slowly rising magma became too much, she promoted herself to captain and was the first one to launch. Captain Susi went on her rocket journey. Her gas and liquid friends joined her. They were all eager to get out. "What will the world be like there?" she wondered. They had heard of earth's surface before, but nobody knew anyone who had been there. "I will be the first one," she said proudly. A true explorer! She was not worried at all. "What could possibly go wrong?" she thought. "This will be pure adventure and fun."

The day finally came. The pressures at the top of the magma chamber were extremely high. Everybody was huffing and puffing. Fueled by a raging mix of gases, Susi and her gang started to climb. First slowly, then, as pressure became higher and higher, they climbed faster and faster. For a moment, Susi had second thoughts. "This is scary," she thought, "but it is too laaaate . . ." Like pop shooting out of a shaken can, the gases exploded way up into the sky. They kept climbing, building up a big cloud of gas and minerals that reached more than ten kilometers into the sky—way above ordinary rain clouds.

Captain Susi spun and spiraled and tried to orient herself in the cloud. "That must be earth's surface down there." The clouds below her blocked her view, but she made out the large **volcano**. Her volcano. It looked pretty beaten up. "I think we did some damage there," she admitted, looking shamefully at the large **crater** she and her gang had left behind. Otherwise, earth's surface was very blue. She realized this must be water and she was above the ocean. "I was born in an island volcano," she said, astonished. Now she was even more relieved that she was high up in the air. This way, she could continue her journey and see a bit more of the world. An island would have been too small for an explorer like Susi.

As Captain Susi climbed with the volcanic cloud, everybody calmed down. The temperature dropped the higher they climbed. The magma that was carried along was shocked and transformed into tiny pieces of glass. Everybody cooled off a bit as the cloud expanded more and more. "What a fantastic day this is," Susi muttered. Being so high up in the sky, she suddenly realized they were being carried by a new force. Strong winds pushed Susi and the entire cloud east and north. "Just when I thought I had everything under control!" Susi thought.

The wind pushed them along for a couple of days, carrying the **ash** cloud for hundreds of kilometers, maybe thousands. Susi didn't keep a record of all she saw, but she does remember when, on the eastern horizon, she suddenly spotted land. Big land. "Canada!" she shouted. "That would be a good place to land." Everyone agreed, but once again, things didn't go according to plan.

That night, a big thunderstorm developed. Strong winds pushed down on Susi's cloud, forcing everyone to fall. It was a scary night with lightning and thunder all around them. Susi tried to navigate through, but she kept getting hit by large raindrops. They lost elevation fast, and soon it became clear they would not make it to Canada. "Prepare for water landing," Susi shouted to everyone. *Splash*—she crashed into the ocean. Her friends followed. The heavy rain continued for hours, but eventually, the weather calmed down and the sun came out.

For a couple more days, Susi and her volcanic ash friends floated at the surface of the ancient ocean. The waves rocked them slowly up and down. "That is not bad," she admitted. "It's actually quite pleasant." Susi and the others enjoyed the calm sea, watching the purple sky changing as the sun rose and set every day on the ocean. During the night, they counted the millions of stars in the sky.

One by one, Susi's friends disappeared, sinking into the ocean. "I am strong!" she yelled angrily at the ocean. "I don't want to go down." The daylight disappeared slowly as she sunk deeper and deeper into the ocean, eventually settling on the muddy ocean bed. Together with her ash friends, they formed a thin blanket of tuff. It was dark down there and the water was calm.

Very slowly, other small minerals settled on top of them. It took a long time. Millions of years. She could not see anything, but she could feel the pressure on her. It also got warmer. "This is too boring for me," Susi declared and decided to fall asleep. "Wake me up if something interesting happens," she said. She took a long nap. A 300-million-year snooze.

She woke to rumbling thunder. Susi looked around. She was shocked. "What's wrong with me?" she wondered, trying to move. "I am glued in this position. Permanently attached to my ash friends?" She became more and more angry as she woke up and tried to move. "I like my friends, but this is too much. I am Captain Susi Sanidine," she yelled. "I am a great explorer! I am independent! A leader! I cannot be glued to anyone!"

But that was her new place in life. There was no time for complaining. The question was, what was that rumbling? The earth was shaking. She looked around. There were soft black shale rocks above and below her. Then she realized her own tuff layer was not much harder. "We are even softer than the shales," she admitted unwillingly. Suddenly, together with the shales, the whole rock layer moved up and tilted. They also moved east somehow; Susi realized. Her navigation skills were still working!

"That could be good," she thought. "Maybe this will finally bring me to Canada." What Susi did not know is that Canada had grown over time, and they were already part of it—just deep below the surface.

The rumbling, tilting, and lifting went on for a while until the world came to a halt again. What happened? It was Mr. McConnell **Thrust**, who carried Captain Susi and her entire neighborhood on his back, moving them all to the east. While thrusting, they got tilted to the west. That's where they ended up about 50 million years ago. And they have stayed there ever since.

Over her long and exciting life, Captain Susi became more patient, but after the tilting, she became hopeful something exciting would happen to her. "It would be great to get to earth's surface again," she thought dreamingly. She wondered how it would be. After all, she had never been on land! Just on the ocean and in the air. Her dream came true! Slowly, the load of rocks above her fell away. Her surroundings became lighter. She could feel it. This process of unloading seemed to have sped up a couple thousand years ago. The glaciers and, lately, the river helped dig her and her shale neighborhood out of the depths. The river formed a valley and carved Jura Creek canyon. When Susi saw the daylight again, she was overjoyed. "Hello world—here I am again," she shouted cheerfully. She looked around and was pleased to see she was on land. Not just boring land, she was in a very pretty Rocky Mountain valley. "This must be Canada," she realized. "We finally landed in Canada!" she yelled at her tuff friends. "I knew we would make it here one day."

This is how Susi and her tuff friends ended up at the bottom of Jura Creek canyon today. They are surrounded by layers of gray **carbonate** below and above them. These layers are much stronger than the 10-meter-thick shale layer where Susi lives. Susi herself has changed. She weathered into a soft yellow mush. Her sanidine crystal changed into the soft **kaolinite** mineral. Her sanidine crystal was not made for life at the surface.

"I get it," she admits. "The shale rocks are the reason I am at the surface now." The river picked this place to form a valley because the shale is weak. Carving out the weaker rocks is easier than carving out the carbonates. The carbonates are hard and strong guys formed by Lucy **Calcite**'s family. "The river is clever," Susi thinks, "taking the easy way to make a big impression on the landscape." Susi acknowledges this strategic decision. "But wait!" she continues her thoughts. "Maybe the shales planned this all a long time ago? Three hundred and sixty million years ago! Building a mountain valley was their master plan and the river was just their tool!"

For now, she decides not to worry and to enjoy her life in the canyon. Over millions of years, Susi has learned to be more patient. "Change will happen—it always does," she thinks hopefully while looking at Jura Creek. "I can't wait to get flushed down the creek and travel again," Susi tells her tuff friends. "Are you guys ready?"

# SCIENCE FACTS

**Ash** – A volcanic ash comprises minerals, rock fragments, and volcanic glass that was ejected during a volcanic eruption together with gas. The ash is carried in large clouds before it rains out to be deposited on the ground. Because the ash material is very light, the big cloud gets carried away with the wind and can travel hundreds and thousands of kilometers. Ash layers are very common in sedimentary rocks, and they can have a thickness of centimeters to meters.

**Calcite** – A mineral, also called calcite carbonate, with the chemical formula of $CaCO_3$. Most calcite carbonate forms thick sediment layers in oceans.

**Carbonate** – A rock type composed of carbonate minerals such as calcite or dolomite. Most of the big cliff-forming rock layers you can see in the Rocky Mountains are carbonates. For example, Cascade Mountain, Castle Mountain, or Mount Yamnuska.

**Crater** – A large hole or depression on the top of a volcano mountain. A crater is formed where the magma explodes out of the volcano. Craters can range very much in size and change in shape and location every time there is a volcanic eruption.

**Crystallized** – The process of forming a solid mineral from a liquid mix of chemical elements is called crystallization. Atoms of various elements bond to each other in a very specific way, forming a regular frame where each atom has its distinct position. The resulting structure is called a mineral crystal.

**Kaolinite** – A very soft and pale or yellow-colored mineral that forms through the breakdown of feldspar minerals such as sanidine. It has the formula $Al_2Si_2O_5(OH)$. Kaolinite is an example of a mineral that forms at or near earth's surface, unlike other minerals that form deep below the surface where it is hotter, and pressures are high.

**Magma** – A mixture of liquid rock material, solid mineral crystals, and gas bubbles. Magma occurs in kilometer-big magma chambers; large bodies of hot and soft rock material located several kilometers below the surface. Many minerals are formed and grow in magma chambers due to slow cooling, a process called crystallization.

**Sanidine** – A potassium silicate mineral with the formula $KAlSi_3O_8$. Sanidine is a feldspar mineral, which is the most common mineral group on continents. Sanidine forms at very high temperatures in the magma in comparison to other feldspar minerals.

**Shale** – A sedimentary rock type that forms in an ocean or a lake. It is composed of very fine mineral grains, mostly clays, and can contain organic material such as algae. The organic material colors the rocks black, giving it the name black shale. Shale rock can be also gray, brown, red, or greenish in color. There is a thick layer of black shale here at the upper Jura Creek. Look for a 2–3 cm thin layer of lighter color that is very soft. That is the ash layer of Susi.

**Thrust** – One of the three types of faults and the most common type you can see in the Rocky Mountains. Old rocks from deep below are thrusted on top of younger rocks. The glide surface that forms is the thrust fault. Thrusting occurs when a region is under compression from the sides, resulting in stacking up layers.

**Tuff** – A rock type. It forms from material that came from a volcano and flew through the air before settling on the ground. Tuff layers can be just a few millimeters thin and up to several meters thick. The chemical composition of a tuff is like a fingerprint and can be traced back to specific volcanoes. This tracing back allows scientists to find out which volcano produced the tuff and in what direction the winds were blowing a long time ago.

**Volcano** – A mountain that sits on top of a magma chamber. It is built by magma that comes from deep below the surface and either flows or shoots out of the volcano, building a mountain.

# SAM COAL
Quarry Lake west of Canmore

Sam

Location: Quarry Lake, Canmore
51.076026°N, 115.373154°W

$S$am lives just below the surface here behind Quarry Lake. He sits in the darkness, squeezed together by the surrounding **sandstone** layers, waiting for something to happen. He has been sitting here for a long time. "Waiting for what?" he sometimes wonders, not knowing if change will be for better or worse. "What is my purpose?" he often questions. "It seems so hard to figure it out."

Sam grew up in this region about 140 million years ago, but, unlike the others around, not as a mineral. Sam used to be something completely different—a beautiful green tree with large leaves to breathe in the fresh sea air. Back then, in the Early Cretaceous, he could see mountains only in the far distance to the west. Sam lived near the sea in a flat coastal region. "I was part of a big forest," he remembers, "and all my friends around me looked just like me—strong and majestic." Together, they elegantly swayed their tree heads in the coastal breeze, day in and day out. They didn't care about anyone else but themselves. "I do remember the dinosaurs!" he thinks. "I never thought I would miss them." Those creatures ate a lot, including trees, but overall, they were entertaining for Sam and his friends.

Like most trees, Sam was brought up to expect an upright life that would end in a slow decay on the forest floor. Sam's purpose was to feed the next generation of trees, like his parents and grandparents did: a meaningful cycle of life. But one night, his life took a different turn. He was in his prime years, standing tall and proud, when it all changed. It was a dark stormy night. Huge ocean waves surged far onto the shores that were battered by rain. The wind became stronger and stronger, shaking Sam and his friends back and forth. Eventually, the wind became too strong for Sam and his trunk broke. He hit the ground with a loud crash.

"Oh no, no, no," Sam screamed as he heard his neighbor tree falling too, landing on top of him. Sam woke up in the dark and realized that something was wrong. "This is not how I expected the ground to be!" he mumbled. "Is that—water? I am lying in water!" His yell got muffled. He realized his roots were mostly wet. He had just never paid attention to it. He lived in a swamp. The view over the beautiful sea was always easier and more enjoyable. "Who looks down at what's underneath you if the views in front are so pretty?" Sam wondered defensively. Suddenly, he regretted his ignorance of the rising water levels and wondered what this unexpected situation meant for him. "Will I be able to decay and nourish the next generation of trees?"

Today, Sam looks around at his tree friends from the Early Cretaceous times. They went through a lot together. They had to go through major changes. Changes that turned them from green, living trees to hard black rocks called **coal**. "I am still alive," he thinks quietly, "it's just a different way of life. The life of a rock." Above and below, trillions of grains of Bob **Quartz's** family hold Sam and the other coals in a tight grip.

When Sam ended up lying underwater, his life took a different path. He could not breathe underwater; no bugs or worms wanted to live in the swamp to help him decay. So, he did not. He was just hanging out, waiting. A large pile of trees crashed down on him. "At least I am not alone in this situation," Sam thought, slightly relieved. "Maybe someone has a clue what will happen to us." Sam looked around, searching. He noticed sand on his head. The water flushed more and more sand grains on top of the dead trees. "These hardworking rivers," Sam thought, "always clearing out the loose rocks from the mountains and dumping it in the sea. They are like an army of cleaners coming to your home." Sam had noticed rivers before when he was a standing tree, but he did not give much attention to what they were really doing. For him, they were just winding pathways of water, pretty to look at. Now he feels their work. Over the next millions of years, the rivers kept transporting more and more grains to the swamp and the sea, adding layers of **mineral** grains on top of Sam. Sam slowly fell asleep.

"I must have slept for a long time." Sam woke up. "One of those million-year-long naps that minerals like to do." Sam wondered where he was. It was still dark around him, but everything felt much tighter and stiffer. His body seemed smaller. The sediment layers on top of him grew thicker and thicker, compressing him. All water was squeezed out. It was warm, very warm. "What is that stink?" Sam looked disgusted. He sniffed around until the realization dawned on him: "It's me. I stink. Me and the other trees!" Sam suddenly became quiet. Looking around, he recognized that all the other former trees had the same shameful look. They were the source of pollution here. "But for what? Is that my new purpose in life? Being stinky?" A hard, black, stinky piece of coal.

As millions of years passed, Sam Coal struggled to accept his new look and smell. He used to be the strong and tall guy, but now he was much weaker and trapped between **sediment** layers. The heat and pressure caused everyone to change into rocks. "But why did I not get stronger, like the sandstones next to me?"

Things also changed outside of his neighborhood. It was in the Late Cretaceous that he first heard rumbling noises from the west. He was not sure what it was, but he recognized that it was increasing. Sam and the rest of the coal layer got scared. Was there another change happening? Even the sandstones above and below them became nervous about the rumbling noise.

Suddenly, the ground shook! And shook again. And another time. Sam tried to yell over the thundering noise. "What is that?" It seemed to come from everywhere now. In that moment, the whole neighborhood was lifted up and squeezed from the side. A big unknown force from the west pushed against them, trying to bend and fold them up like a giant burrito. The newly formed Rocky Mountains pushed from the west to grow eastward. Sam quickly realized this was his moment to prove he could be helpful.

"I think we need to help our sandstone neighbors," he shouted to his coal friends around him, trying to be heard by everyone. "They are too brittle to be folded up. They will break if we don't do anything. We are softer and malleable." The coals agreed to help and started to move. They slowly relocated into the tight corner of the fold so the sandstone would have to bend less. The motion of the coals made it easier for the sandstones to bend over and find a new home position without breaking. This migration and bending went on for a couple million years. It was thanks to the coals that many sandstone layers survived.

About 70 million years ago, the shaking stopped. A heavy load rested on the coal beds. What happened? A large **thrust fault** from the west had emerged and run over the neighborhood carrying a thick package of rocks on top of them. Indeed, it was

Mr. Rundle Thrust who pushed from below and dragged part of Sam's neighborhood along as he aimed up and eastward. This dragging caused the entire neighborhood to fold onto itself—burrito style. On his back, Mr. Rundle carried a kilometer-thick slab of very old rocks, burdening Sam's folded neighborhood even more. Some shaking and rumbling continued for another 20 million years until everything became quiet again.

After that, Sam felt much better about being a coal. "I can be more than just a smelly neighbor," he thought. There was a mutual respect now. The sand grains acknowledged what the coals did for them. Sam started to appreciate minerals more and more. "They are kind of cool little guys," he admitted, "and there is such a great variety among them." He mumbled softly, "I am more like them now. I am a rock."

The load of Mr. Rundle and his limestone backpack wore hard on everyone in Sam's neighborhood. The pressure and the heat had increased and stayed a long time. Over the next tens of millions of years, not much happened. Eventually, Sam and his friends realized the overburden had lifted, and the heat declined. Rivers and glaciers on top of Sam removed the rocks at the surface, slowly excavating the neighborhood. "Look at me—I am shiny." Sam was surprised that his dull black color had turned into an elegant dark silver. "Am I getting old?" he wondered. "Whatever it is, I like my **anthracitic** look." He turned not just into ordinary coal, but coal of high grade. He looked desirable. Soon he learned that he and his friends were desired by others too.

Less than a hundred years ago now, the neighborhood turned noisy again. He heard it, and others did too. It was not as loud and forceful as the thrusting during the Cretaceous times of mountain building, but it was still audible to the entire region. Word spread that creatures living at earth's surface were digging up their neighborhood. Apparently, these creatures were after him. They left the sandstone layers behind but mined out the coals. "What does that mean for me?" Sam wondered. "Do I want those creatures to find me?" Sam pondered the possible consequences. After all, he was born to fuel the next generations of trees. But this seemed different. "Who are these surface creatures anyway?" he wondered, slightly annoyed. "Dinosaurs?" The mining noise had vanished a couple decades ago and Sam is happy he survived undiscovered. He feels there will be better opportunities to be useful.

# SCIENCE FACTS

*Anthracitic* – The coal that has experienced high temperature is called anthracite. It is harder than other coals and has a glossy dark silver appearance that is called anthracitic.

*Coal* – A rock composed of mostly organic material deposited in water. It is therefore a sedimentary rock and appears in layers between other sediments such as sandstone or shale. Coal has been used as fuel for thousands of years.

*Fault* – A surface that forms when rocks break into two parts that then move in different ways. Faults can be between a few square meters and hundreds of square kilometers big. There are three types of faults: (1) normal faults form when earth's crust is stretched and rocks slide down from another; (2) thrust faults form when earth's crust is pressed together and rocks slide on top of each other; (3) strike-slip faults form when earth's crust is teared and one side moves in the opposite direction to the other side, causing the rocks to move along each other.

**Mineral** – The building blocks of rocks. Minerals are composed of various chemical elements that build specific crystal structures. Minerals vary in their grain size from a few micrometers to millimeters; only sometimes do they grow to centimeter sizes.

**Quartz** – A mineral composed of silica oxide, $SiO_2$. Quartz is a very common mineral and forms large portions of rocks like granite, sandstones, or quartzite. The cliffs at the back of Lake Louise are quartzite rocks. They are composed almost entirely of quartz that was hardened by high temperatures and pressures when they were buried kilometers below earth's surface.

**Sandstone** – A sedimentary rock composed of sand-size mineral grains that were deposited in an ocean, lake, riverbed, or sand dune. The loose sand is transformed into sandstone by overburden and heat due to rock layers deposited on top of the sand over millions of years. Sandstones are mostly composed of quartz grains.

**Sediment** – Material that is transported by wind, water, or glaciers and deposited in layers in low-lying areas. Most sediment is transported from mountainous regions into oceans. The process of sedimentation continuous for millions of years, building up kilometers of thick layers of sediment. The deep burial of sediment transforms it into sedimentary rocks.

**Thrust** – One of the three types of faults and the most common type you can see in the Rocky Mountains. Old rocks from deep below earth's surface are thrusted on top of younger rocks at shallower depths. This process occurs when a region is under compression from the sides, resulting in stacking up.

# EMMA AMPHIPORA
Rock wall behind the upper Grassi Lake

Location: Grassi Lake

51.072629°N, 115.406726°W

Scan Me

Emma has lived her entire life here in Western Canada, and although this place has changed a lot, she still loves it. From an early age, Emma knew she wanted to make this world a more beautiful place. She had a strong sense for the arts and design. Architecture was her favorite subject. "I am going to build a city that will last forever," she declared to her parents. "A **coral reef** city that is not just for me, but for all my friends and the generations after me." That was 378 million years ago. It wasn't a total surprise for her parents. This occupation runs in her family. Many of her ancestors were builders and designers, and all of them had a strong sense for functionality and beauty. But Emma wanted more. She wanted her coral reef to last forever. We are not talking about centuries or millennia—we are talking big time! Earth history time.

Emma **Amphipora** was born as an animal. Together with her sponge family, she lived in the warm waters of the ancient Devonian ocean. Here, the water was shallow and crystal clear. Rays of sunlight reached deep down, tickling her. When Emma was not daydreaming and planning her coral reef city, she played with fish and other sea animals.

"One day," Emma said to her fish friends, "I will be a beautiful rock. A rock that is light and airy, but at the same time strong and enduring." To get started, Emma grew a skeleton. This was the first step to building the coral reef that would last forever. "I need a good structural design, but also the right building material." Emma was a bit afraid she would run out of building supplies. After all, her vision was to build a big reef! "I should build something out of ocean water," she said, wondering what exactly was in ocean water. She found out that it was full of

**calcium** and **carbon dioxide**, which she transformed into a solid **calcite** skeleton. "That works," she said, looking proudly at her calcite bones.

For her reef structure, Emma tested a couple designs, aiming to make it durable but also elegant and airy with lots of space for the water to go in and out. She finally came up with a very clever plan. She decided to grow big flat platforms that were stacked on top of each other. In between the platforms she grew pillars, forming large galleries. A beautiful, modern, and cheerful design, all in bright light gray. Over the years, she added layers on top, growing higher and wider. "Let's build a reef city!" she encouraged her neighbors. "We will build the biggest coral reef the ocean has ever seen." And so, they did, all along the shallow underwater banks that used to stretch across the ancient Alberta ocean.

In the beginning, Emma's skeleton was not rock solid. Emma kept the design soft and flexible, allowing her to move with the waves. But over the years, her bones became harder and more brittle. Eventually, Emma transitioned into a rock. A rocky document of her animal life. She could not be happier. Her vision came true. "Now, I will live forever!" was her last thought before her sponge life ended and her rock life started. Her satisfied smile was now **fossilized** in her rock face.

But shortly afterwards, the unthinkable happened. A large storm came. A really big one! Bigger than all the others before. Emma was frightened. "Will this monster destroy my city?" she yelled over the storm. Emma knew that rock cannot bend easily. "I will break!" she panicked "We will all break." Huge waves hammered against the coral reef and broke it into thousands of rock pieces. The fossil skeletons of Emma and her family were dismembered and rolled around. Emma cried hopelessly. "My reef city is destroyed."

When the new day began, the waters calmed down. The coral reef looked like a battlefield. The work of so many years—destroyed overnight. The water was still disturbed and muddy, so sunlight could not reach far into the waters. Animals suffered. Many died. Most of them depended on the sunlight and clear water for drinking. It took years before new animals settled on the rubble, trying to grow a new reef.

And Emma? Broken apart and lying in a strange position made her feel even more uncomfortable. As she tried to look around, she realized everybody had the same problem. "We are not gone," Emma thought with a glimpse of hope. Over the years, Emma tried to focus on the fact that her coral reef still existed, just not how she envisioned it. It now had a look of destruction and waste.

As the next generations of reef animals grew on top of Emma's broken city, the sunlight became more and more rare for her to see. "That's what it means to be a rock," Emma realized, "they mostly live in the darkness." She usually avoided surprises with careful research and planning. "I should have predicted this," she said, wondering what else she may have overlooked in her master plan. "I can do this. I can adapt," she decided. After all, she had always wanted to be a rock. So, she didn't complain.

Emma tried to make the best out of this situation. Her reef city was heavily damaged, but it was still there! She started to question if her calcite skeleton would be strong enough to sustain whatever came next. The load from the top seemed to become heavier every year as the younger generations of coral reefs grew bigger. "Maybe I need to make my skeleton stronger." Emma started to replace some of the calcium with **magnesium**. "Magnesium supplements are always good to become stronger and harder," she thought as she turned her calcite structure into **dolomite**. That's right, dolomite was the new fancy way to design strong buildings. Even though her platform and pillar structures were not horizontal anymore, Emma wanted to do everything she could to prevent her reef city from vanishing.

The plan worked out. Emma's Devonian city is still standing today, just behind the upper Grassi Lake. Like most people in Canmore, Emma is happy living here. The location is perfect. Plenty of sunlight, close to the water, and the view is spectacular. But it took a long time for Emma to come back to earth's surface.

After Emma lost the sunlight entirely in the Devonian time, she entered a long period of waiting. "That's what rocks are good at—waiting." She tried to stay focused and patient. But what was she waiting for? The kilometers of rock layers above her became heavier and heavier. In fact, the load smushed the city together even more. "This is a fossil graveyard of my coral reef," she thought, slightly depressed. "Nobody wants to live here or look at it." But Emma was wrong.

She does not remember when exactly she noted it first, but one day, she felt different. "Is it possible," she wondered, "a rock can smell?" With time, the changes became more obvious. An oily odor became stronger and stronger, and suddenly, the dolomite structure felt slippery. The light-colored galleries slowly filled with **crude oil**. It was dark brown, smelly oil. Emma was astonished. "What is that?" She wondered what to make out of this invasion. The oil stained her light gray reef city as it moved quickly, soon occupying all the rooms that Emma once crafted so carefully. "You are welcome." She pretended to be a good host, still wondering how she felt about the oily newcomers. "I built this city for you," she said, realizing that the oil didn't mind the broken pieces. "Maybe that was what I was waiting for," Emma muttered to herself. She felt happy to have found an unexpected purpose for her coral reef.

It was about 72 million years ago when suddenly, the reef city shook with a strong push coming from the west. The pressure was strong, and for other rock layers above and below her, the pushing was unbearable. But not for Emma. The oil in her reef galleries protected her from being squeezed too hard. "Finally, someone is on my side," Emma cheered. But then it came. She felt the lift. It was Mr. Rundle **Thrust fault** who broke through underneath her and lifted one side of the reef up and over to the east. "Ha ha—that's fun," Emma said loudly. Although, she realized her entire reef city was now inclined, dipping steeply to the west.

Just in that moment, a big loud quake rattled the earth. "What's that?" Emma screamed, realizing this was not Mr. Rundle below her. Something else had happened right next to her. A huge crack formed. A vertical fault cut through her city and all the neighborhoods above her. Cautiously, she waited. The rumbling and breaking continued before vanishing slowly over the next millions of years. Some portions of her reef city were destroyed even more. Some of the oil left, dripped away. Emma desperately wondered if that was the fate of her city, to become more and more ruined.

Once again, the disaster of faulting turned out to have a positive side as well. The vertical fault helped create a valley—a valley that eventually exposed Emma to daylight. A couple thousand years ago, the **erosion** carved deep enough to expose her reef rocks to the sunlight. That was the happiest day of her life.

"Whoa," Emma yelled, full of astonishment when she saw the sun again. Looking around, she realized how different this place looked. Growing up as a sponge in the ocean, she had never seen land before! And what a land this is! There are mountain peaks and valleys. Looking around makes her realize there are many other rock layers that are also not horizontal. On the contrary, the rock layers all dip in different directions. "Maybe this is the style now," she thinks. "In this case, my city fits right in." She looks at her city with pride and satisfaction.

# SCIENCE FACTS

*Amphipora* – An animal belonging to the group of ancient sponges called Stromatoporoids. They lived from the Ordovician time until their extinction in the Early Carboniferous. The Devonian time was the peak period for these animals. During the Devonian, a large reef stretched across the shallow ocean that occupied Alberta. These reef rocks are the main reservoir rock for oil found in the province.

*Calcite* – A mineral composed of calcium carbonate $CaCO_3$. Rocks composed mostly of calcite minerals are called carbonate rocks or limestones. Most of the cliff-forming mountain peaks in the Rocky Mountains are composed of limestone.

**Calcium** – A chemical element with the formula Ca. Calcium is built into many minerals such as calcite ($CaCO_3$) that compose most of the rocks in the Rocky Mountains. Calcite is easily dissolved in water and can be transported away. Similarly, calcium easily bonds with other atoms to form minerals such as calcite.

**Carbon dioxide** – A gas with the chemical formula $CO_2$. The $CO_2$ molecule consists of one carbon atom bonded to two oxygen atoms. It occurs naturally in the atmosphere and dissolves in water.

**Coral reef** – An underwater structure built of corals and sponges that form large carbonate structures. They are important places for many life forms and mostly occur in shallow and tropical waters. The first reefs formed 485 million years ago in the Ordovician time.

**Crude Oil** – A naturally occurring oil that originates from dead organisms that are deposited on the ocean floor together with other mineral grains. Heating of the sediment due to deep burial turns the organic material into oil. Oil is a mix of hydrogen (H) and carbon (C) atoms, called hydrocarbons. When oil forms in the rock, it moves into other rock layers where it fills small spaces.

**Dolomite** – A mineral composed of calcium magnesium carbonate with the formula $CaMg(CO_3)$. It does not rapidly dissolve like calcium carbonate.

**Erosion** – The process of removing rock from earth's surface. There are many forces that cause erosion, such as the power of glaciers, rivers, ocean waves, or strong winds.

**Fault** – A surface that splits a rock and moves one side in a different direction than the other side of the rock. Looking at a rock cliff, a fault usually looks like a line separating the two rock units. Faults can vary in size depending on how much they move and how long they move for.

**Fossilized** – A rock record of an ancient organism (animal or plant) in the form of an imprint, bones, shells, footprints, or others is called a fossil. Fossils can teach us about the evolution of life over geologic times. They can also tell us about the past environment in which the organism lived (e.g. lake, near the beach, deep ocean). The process of transforming a living organism into a rock record is called fossilization.

**Magnesium** – A chemical element with the formula Mg. Magnesium is the eighth most abundant element on earth and is built into many minerals such as dolomite.

**Thrust** – One of the three types of faults and the most common type you can see in the Rocky Mountains. Old rocks from deep below earth's surface are thrusted on top of younger rocks. This process occurs when a region is under compression from the sides, resulting in stacking up layers.

# DAVID ROCK FLOUR
The color of Moraine Lake

*David*

*Location: Moraine Lake*
*51.327625°N, 116.180422°W*

David floats in Moraine Lake in the warm summer sun. There is nothing that can disrupt his happiness. He has finally arrived at the place he is meant to be. Admired by the world for his bright turquoise color, he is the center of attention, the most beautiful thing on the planet. Everybody wants to see him.

David's journey started 500 million years ago in the blue waters of the ancient ocean that occupied Western Canada. Water has always been his element. He loved swimming around and being seen by others. Back then, he was a small **calcite** grain that eventually settled on the ocean floor together with many other grains. They were the guys that buried Charles **Zircon** and his friend Bob **Quartz**. Like Charles, David was also slowly buried by younger grains that settled on top of him, like Lucy Calcite. Hundreds of millions of years he waited, getting buried deeper and deeper, far away from daylight. Eventually, the kilometer-thick pile of younger grains on top of David turned him and his **mineral** neighbors into a rock. David was not too concerned; he is a pretty laid-back guy. "One day," he was convinced, "I will be back at earth's surface, in the water, and I will make the world beautiful." Patience is David's main strength.

He survived the many million years of heat and pressure, squeezing and hugging. "Ew, I hate hugs," he quietly thought while trying to escape his neighbors. But there was no escape! All grains got pushed closer together with the ever-growing burden of the rock layers above. He just had to suck it up and suffer through it. It takes guts to become a rock! "How long could this possibly last?" he wondered every couple hundred million years. Over time, he tried to adjust to the intense hugging. "I guess they like me," he sometimes pondered. "I should be happy about that." David also tolerated the **earthquake** era when the Rocky Mountains formed and there was lots of shattering and breaking of rock layers around him. "This may be a good sign," he noticed, "a sign that my time to shine will come soon."

However, many more years passed before his dream came true. Nothing happened in these last years—just chilling for another 70 million years or so. But then, suddenly, a grinding and crunching noise! David could hear it only faintly in the distance. But soon, he was sure there was something going on. A constant scraping and grinding at the rocky surface. The noise of a **glacier**, a white pathway that slowly—very slowly—crept down the valley. David couldn't see the glacier because he was still deep below the surface. News about glaciers quickly spread from rock layer to rock layer all the way down to David. "Will the glacier free me from the burden of the other rock layers?" he wondered hopefully.

David was right that he would be freed by the glacier, but that took a couple hundred thousand more years. In that time, the glacier grew and shrunk, grinding off rock layers from the surface. Recently, about 14 thousand years ago, the grinding noise became really loud. Suddenly, David was carved out of his rock layer by the glacier. It was an aggressive glacier belly made of rock pieces frozen into the ice, which together acted like a giant cheese grater. It milled down the rocks from the glacier bed and pushed them down the valley. David said, "Okay, let's go! I have been waiting for you!" And the glacier scaped him off the surface and pushed him gently together with many other rock pieces. His travels didn't last very long though, and David soon found himself stuck in a rock pile halfway down the valley. Some of the rocks in the pile were large, like big boxes, and others were like sand grains or even smaller. David was one of the smallest in the pile. He was about one hundred times smaller than Charles or Bob, tiny and fine like flour. That's when he realized that he was not a solid rock anymore; he became David **Rock Flour**.

"It feels nice to be so small and loose," David thought. "I am finally free from the hugging minerals around me." He hung out in the rock pile for a couple more years, slowly being eroded by the rivers draining out of the melting glacier or formed during summer rains. Over the years, the glacier disappeared more and more, until no ice was visible. David's glacial rock pile was hanging halfway up a valley. "I guess I have to wait a little bit longer," David mumbled. "This is interesting, maybe, for some people, but it is not very pretty." His big day must be close. Maybe next year something would happen.

David was right. That year, it finally happened. As the early summer sun became stronger and stronger, drops of snow melted quickly and turned creeks into small rivers. The water washed out the fine sand and the rock flour, including David. His neighbors had already been carried away the week before, and now it was David's turn. He got flushed down the valley and spilled out into Moraine Lake. "Yippee," David yelled joyfully as he immersed into the water. Because he is so small and light, he floats. The water's motion lifted him in a dance of water and rock flour, like graceful partners swinging up and down, right and left. The sun warmed the water and David just floated and enjoyed life. "Finally, I feel wonderfully light!" he yelled happily. "I can stretch and move in all directions." David realized what he had missed the last 500 million years. "Hello sun—can you see me? I am here."

Soon, he learned from the other rock flour about his new job—their magic job of coloring the lake turquoise. It turns out, it is a pretty easy trick. David just takes all the sunbeams and sorts them according to their waviness. The long beams go to the water and the short beams he swallows, but the medium sunbeams he sends back to the sky. These are the blue and green sunrays, and as they mix, they turn turquoise. That's the trick of rock flour dancing with water. David is incredibly proud to be part of this magic. "Who doesn't want to be a magician," he thinks, "enchanting and beautifying the world?"

David will work for the entire season. It's fun work, but also tiring. His magic time will be over when the frost comes and puts an icy blanket on Moraine Lake. This is when David will be able to rest and retire at the bottom of the lake. What will happen next? More rock flour will settle on top of him. "They will hug me again," he groans, "but it was so worth it." David knows one day he will be back at the surface with a new trick. "It will be beautiful," he thinks confidently. "Until then, I just wait."

# SCIENCE FACTS

*Calcite* – A mineral composed of calcium carbonate $CaCO_3$. Rocks composed mostly of calcite minerals are called carbonate rocks or limestones. Most of the cliff-forming mountain peaks in the Rocky Mountains are composed of limestone.

**Earthquake** – Happens when rocks break on a large scale. During Rocky Mountain building, the rock layers were pushed together from the side, which caused rock layers to break and large faults to form. The breaking process creates an intense shaking of the rocks deep below earth's surface. This shaking is what we call an earthquake. Large earthquakes can be felt by animals and humans at the surface.

**Glacier** – A mass of ice that forms at the high mountain peaks where it is cold and snowy. Like rivers, glaciers flow down the valley, but at a much slower pace. The Rocky Mountains were covered by glaciers over the past 2.6 million years. During that time, glaciers went through several cycles of growing and retreating as the climate shifted to colder and warmer times. We are currently in a warm phase and most glaciers have disappeared. You can still see some remnants of glaciers high up in the mountain, such as behind Lake Louise or on Mount Temple on the road to this location.

**Mineral** – The building blocks of rocks. Minerals are composed of various chemical elements that build specific crystal structures. Minerals vary in their grain size from a few micrometers to millimeters; only sometimes do they grow to centimeter sizes.

**Quartz** – A very common mineral composed of one silicon and four oxygen atoms bonded together: $SiO_4$. Quartz can have many forms and colors, but most quartz grains have no color and appear light gray. Sand and sandstone are mostly composed of quartz grains that were rounded due to transport by rivers or wind.

**Rock Flour** – A rock material that is very fine grained, like flour. You cannot feel the grains when smearing the rock flour between your fingers. Because the grains are so small, they do not sink if the water is not absolutely still.

**Zircon** – A mineral with the formula $ZrSiO_4$ that is very hard and durable. Many rocks contain zircon, but only in very small amounts. Zircon is a silicate mineral with zirconium built into the lattice.

# KAREN WATERDROP
At Many Springs Lake

Karen

Location: Many Springs Lake
in Bow Valley Provincial Park
51.071679°N, 115.114505°W

At the bottom of Many Springs Lake, Karen **Water**drop pushes, presses, and squeezes herself through the sandy grains. Then, she is finally out and swimming in the lake after a thousand years of being underground. She feels free and happy. "What a beautiful little lake this is," she thinks. "I was not sure if I would ever make it to the sunlight again," she admits to the surrounding water friends while smiling at the sun. But once again, Karen has made an appearance on earth's surface. Karen thinks back to the beginning, when she started her journey that would bring her to this lake—all alone.

Karen's not quite sure when and where her story began. She is one of those who looks very young, only a few thousand years old. That is much younger than all the old mineral friends she's met along her journey. At least, that's what she believes and that's what she wants others to believe. The truth is, she is much older—as old as a mineral. Her memory is just really bad, and Karen is an expert in recreating herself. She is constantly changing and reinventing her look. "Who cares about the past?" she says to the other waterdrops in the lake. "I much rather enjoy the now and seeing where life takes me tomorrow." And life has taken her around the globe quite a bit. Karen is well-traveled, very well-traveled, but again, she doesn't remember it all. Her memories erase quickly as she is reborn again and again.

Karen remembers traveling with the wind across the Pacific Ocean, high up in the air. That was one or two thousand years ago. It took several days with only the deep blue ocean below her. "Am I getting anywhere?" she wondered. Suddenly, "Land—there is land," she yelled as she spotted Vancouver Island and the western part of Canada. "Whatever this land is, I hope it is more exciting than this ocean." Karen got lucky, and Canada did not disappoint her. It was pretty, like today, but without the big cities and roads. As she navigated closer to Canada, the Coast Mountains of British Columbia forced the air to move up, higher into the sky. It was much colder up there, and the air lost the power to carry Karen and other water friends. Clouds formed— large white and light gray puffy clouds made of big waterdrops.

The waterdrops were too heavy to move up higher and over the majestic mountain peaks! So, one waterdrop after the other decided to drop out of the cloud and down towards earth. Karen looked down curiously, wondering what Canada was like. "Let's check it out," she decided, and relaxed her body and started falling. "Whoa—that is fast!" At just the moment when Karen thought about her landing, she crashed into a rock. "Ouch!" Slowly, she collected her senses. "Canada is painful," she whined quietly while looking around for shelter from the other rain- drops that followed her. She decided to squeeze into a tiny crack in the rock and wait it out.

Soon after her crash into the rocky peaks of the Coast Mountains, the sun came out. Afraid of missing something excit- ing, Karen decided to leave her shelter. The warm air invited her to get carried away again. "I'll travel a bit further," Karen decided and rose with the warm air to continue her journey eastwards. "The land is beautiful," she noted, looking at the lakes, moun- tains, and forests. Karen quickly got used to crashes as she fell out of the sky a couple more times during her travels. Often, she got lucky and landed gently on a leaf, splashed into soft soil, or into one of the numerous big lakes. Karen would usually spend a couple days on the ground, sometimes even longer.

Karen smiles today thinking about her first crash landing in Canada. Thankfully, she is so flexible and robust. "Once I got sucked up into a tree," Karen proudly tells some of her water friends that swim next to her. "I moved through the whole thing, from the roots all the way up to the leaves. It was wild." But the powerful rays of the sun always got her out and up in the air again.

Months passed and winter came. Not much water was left in the freezing air. That's when something amazing happened to Karen when she was flying over the Rocky Mountains and the foothills. "I feel different, somehow stiff," she thought, slowly looking at herself. "What is that?" She waved around an arm that grew out of her body. In fact, there were six arms. Confused, she looked around and realized all the other waterdrops had turned into little crystals with long arms. "They look beautiful. I am beautiful! I am an ice crystal."

Karen had heard of this transformation before but had never gone through it herself. Or maybe she had, but she didn't remember. Karen felt even lighter as a snowflake. Playing with the wind, she was pushed up and down. The other snowflakes started to fall towards the ground. "No, no, no—not that fast! I first want to dance and play a little." Another snowflake took her arms and they started to dance. "This frosty new friend clearly knows the moves," Karen thought, impressed, and happily followed her new friend's lead. For a while, they danced elegantly through the wintery mountain, until they gently settled on the ground.

Over the next hours, more and more snowflakes settled on top of her. It felt good and fuzzy. Everybody was so light, not really a burden. It even felt like the neighboring snowflakes kept her warm. Several months of darkness and stillness passed. It was not an easy time for Karen. After all, she was used to moving all the time. Before, the sun would always help her, but now, she could not see the sun anymore. "Am I stuck here forever?" Eventually, spring came and the sun warmed up the foothills. The ice crystals melted and turned into water again. But this time, Karen's journey took a different direction. The spring sun was not strong enough to lift everybody up in the air, so some waterdrops stayed behind and got drawn into the ground. That's what happened to Karen. Gravity pulled her into earth. "Let's see what's down in the underground. It must be dark and mysterious there."

After a short journey through the soil and roots, she ended up in a thick **sandstone** layer. "It's not really that cold here." Karen was surprised and started to follow the sandy layer deeper and deeper and towards the west. It was like a long staircase. She could only move slowly. The spaces between the sandy **mineral** grains became smaller as they were pressed more closely together with the growing overburden. "It's not easy to move in a rock," Karen realized. Her explorer spirit kept her going. "I can't wait to see what's at the end of the sandstone layer deep down." However, sometimes she wondered how far she could go before she would get stuck entirely. The tricky part was to move from one little open space between the mineral grains to the next.

At first, she ignored those old minerals dudes. They seemed to only block her way, slowing her down, and she did not want to deal with them at all. It took a couple years until she got to know them better. She had to admit that some of them were quite interesting looking. Most of the mineral grains she met were from Bob **Quartz**'s family, but she also met a few others like those from Jenny **Apatite**'s family. The underground mineral world was not only dark, it was also slow. "Everyone is so laid-back down here." Karen was amazed. Over time, she adapted to the slow pace of life. It allowed her to experience the moments in a more profound way.

Karen started to nicely ask each grain to allow her to squeeze around them into the next little open space. Sometimes this was easily done, and she made good progress on her journey deeper down the sandstone layer, but sometimes it took longer. She would hang out with some grains and chat for a while until Karen found a way to keep moving to the next open space. "These minerals have such long stories to tell." Karen was fascinated. As she moved slowly deeper, it became even warmer. Although she missed the sunlight, this underground mineral world fascinated her. "I should enjoy it as long as it lasts," she thought, knowing that one day, it would change again.

That day came sooner than expected. Her underground travel lasted for a thousand years or so, when suddenly, the sandstone layer ended. Her first clue was when the open spaces became larger, and her moves became easier. Cracks showed up in the rock, allowing her to move quickly. Suddenly, a lot of other water-drops surrounded her. It was a **fault zone**, but not just any fault zone. Karen had moved into the middle of the McConnell **thrust** fault. It was a meter-thick layer of rock chaos and lots of water that did not know where to go. Crushed up grains and newly formed minerals such as from the extended family of Joel **Illite** lived in the fault zone. On the other side of the fault zone were entirely different rocks, ones who weren't good for traveling through, but Mr. McConnell Thrust himself appeared to be a perfect travel path. He was a pipe, a pipe that would transport Karen up to the surface again. As more and more waterdrops came together here, the pressure increased. Karen found herself in an upward flow along the thrust fault. "Here we go again!" Karen was excited to feel that a new, accelerated phase of her life was about to start. Quickly, she said goodbye to her mineral friends. She was now among many other waterdrops. "I am not even a waterdrop anymore. I am part of a larger flowing water body."

Shortly after, Karen squeezed out of the ground at the bottom of Many Springs Lake. "Hello sun. I am here again!" She swam happily together with the other water friends. "I am a lake now," she thought, slightly surprised that she was enjoying the feeling of being a part of a larger body. "I like to do my own thing, but this is also nice—for now."

Today, Karen feels change is about to happen. "I think we are all going on a journey together." Karen is excited and takes the lead swimming towards the outlet of the lake. She recently heard about the nearby Bow River, a large mountain river that flows eastwards. "I heard there is a lot more of Canada to see east of us," she enthusiastically tells her friends. "I am ready to go on a new journey with the river. Let's keep exploring."

# SCIENCE FACTS

*Apatite* – A mineral that is mostly composed of calcium and phosphate: $Ca_5(PO_4)_3(F,Cl,OH)$. Like zircon, apatite is commonly found in many rocks, but in very small amounts.

**Fault zone** – The area around the fault plane where the rocks are broken and deformed due to the rock motion. Large faults such as the McConnell thrust have a fault zone that is several meters thick. The broken rocks in a fault zone allow water to move through and new minerals to grow during the faulting processes.

**Illite** – A mineral that belongs to the group of clay minerals. It is composed of layers of silica with water and other elements loosely located between the layers. Because of the layered structure, these minerals are also called phyllosilicate. The chemical formula of illite is quite long and shows that various atoms can be built in between the layers and exchanged easily: $(K,H_3O)(Al,Mg,Fe)_2(Si,Al)_4O_{10}[(OH)_2,(H_2O)]$.

**Mineral** – The building blocks of rocks. Minerals are composed of various chemical elements that build specific crystal structures.

**Quartz** – A mineral composed of silica oxide $SiO_2$. Quartz is a very common mineral and forms large portions of rocks like granite, sandstones, or quartzite.

**Sandstone** – A sedimentary rock type composed of sand-size mineral grains that were deposited in an ocean, lake, riverbed, or sand dune. The loose sand was transformed into sandstone by overburden and heat due to rock layers deposited on top of the sand over millions of years.

**Thrust** – One of the three types of faults and the most common type you can see in the Rocky Mountains. Old rocks from deep below earth's surface are thrusted on top of younger rocks. This process occurs when a region is under compression from the sides, resulting in stacking up layers.

**Water** – A molecule comprising one oxygen and two hydrogen atoms; the chemical formula is $H_2O$. Water is the fluid form. Water freezes below 0°C and forms ice. At high temperatures, water evaporates and becomes a gas. Changes in temperature and pressure cause water to constantly change its form and its location, ranging from the air, the surface, and deep below earth's surface. Water can also be part of a mineral such as Joel Illite.

# PETER PEBBLE
Centennial Ridge

Peter

Location: Ribbon Creek Parking Lot
50.932697°N, -115.148479°W

Scan Me

**P**eter is a real nerd: observing, documenting, and analyzing data. Every day, Peter looks curiously over the Kananaskis Valley. Here, from Centennial Ridge, he has a good view down to the river and up to the peaks. He estimates the snow cover on the mountaintops. He then continues checking the migrating birds and the wildlife in the valley. Recently, he has also begun checking the car traffic on the highway. He records every change: changes from yesterday, last week, last year, the last million years. "Data is so much fun!" He smiles while making mental notes. "It allows me to understand the world and predict the future." That is Peter's world. It gives him comfort and helps him deal with change because there is always change. That's what Peter is sure about.

Peter's own life has been full of change. He was born during the Carboniferous, a time of big changes. His story started about 340 million years ago. In the ancient ocean that occupied Western Canada, thick layers of mud settled on the seabed. This mud was a mixture of fine ground-up rocks from the old **craton** in the east, algae, and dead ocean creatures along with their skeletons and shells. Most of these shells and skeletons were tiny— micrometer small. These microstructures were really popular back in the ancient ocean and were made of either **calcite** or **silica** material. Over time, hundreds of meters of muddy stuff settled on the seafloor. This heavy load squished the material together and it became warmer with every meter it was buried deeper. During these times, the little silica skeletons dissolved in water and started to move around in the neighborhood.

"Let's get together and form our own community," the silica said. "We are otherwise outnumbered by the calcite that is everywhere." So, the silica decided to migrate to places where they could live together, forming silica islands within the many calcites. Turns out that the smell of the dead ocean creatures was very attractive to silica and guided their migration. "The chemistry is just right here," the silica decided and crystallized. It formed ball-like knobs and wobbly layers of centimeter thickness. This is how Peter **Chert** was born, in a silica knob in the middle of a very thick **limestone** layer. This whole **diagenetic** process slowly transformed the soft mud into stiff rock.

Peter's desire for data was not always as strong as it is today. It grew over time. "My youth was rather boring," Peter often says, "but the dull surroundings of the first 200 million years of my life sharpened my senses to detect even little changes." Back then, he was trapped in the rock layer kilometers below earth's surface. Peter did not even know there was a surface, sun, sky, and all that. It was dark and tight all around him. The only data he was able to collect was the weight on top of him and how warm it was.

One day, in the Late Jurassic period, Peter detected a change. "I feel someone pushing from my western side," he told his friends, wondering if they noticed it too. "Yes, I am sure something is going on. I can also hear it." Peter was excited and recorded the pressure from the west and the sounds. This went on for millions of years until, suddenly, the world seemed to collapse. Rumbling and rattling below him became stronger and stronger. His entire rock layer started to break into large and small pieces. "What is going on?" Peter screamed. Everyone was surprised though—the chert knobs as much as the calcite neighborhood. The rattling, cracking, and shaking went on for a while, breaking more and more of the neighborhood apart.

Suddenly, they were lifted up. The heavy load from the over-burdened rock layers became less and less every year. "That feels nice," Peter thought as he recognized the lightness of his surroundings. Big change was clearly happening. This was when Peter became much more serious about data. He now started to record the pressure, the noise, the shaking, and cracking. How did they change from one day to the next? He not only found the daily data collection very interesting, it also calmed him down. "At least I am doing something," he thought. "I cannot ignore the change. If I have enough data, I may be able to predict the future."

Within only a few million years, Peter and his rocky neighborhood were lifted up to the surface by a large **thrust fault** that lay underneath them. The most exciting day in Peter's life was yet to come. From his data, Peter knew there was not much rock above him. "I cannot feel any weight," he said to his chert friends, wondering what that meant. In that moment, a crack formed and split the rock just in front of him. As the one side fell down the mountain slope, Peter was exposed to the sun. "This is too bright," he shouted into the air. Slowly, he adjusted to this new and seemingly harsh environment. He carefully looked around—and was speechless. Who would have known this existed? "How can I ever document it all?" he thought. "There is so much going on. But it's definitively not boring! I love the earth's surface!"

Today at Centennial Ridge, Peter smiles as he thinks back to these first days at the surface. "That was one of the best times in my life. I made up new words every day. I had to. There were just so many unknown objects. Mountains, rivers, trees, and all kinds of animals." Peter looks down at the Kananaskis Village. "The animals looked quite different back then. Some were really big. Dinosaurs we called them." Peter squints, trying to count the cars on highway 40. "There are just too many things going on these days," he mutters, slightly annoyed about the fast-moving cars that mess up his data collection. "Did I already count this one?"

Back in the Early Cretaceous, Peter's time at the exposed rock cliff did not last long, maybe a couple hundred years. Because the calcite was easily washed away, the strong chert communities were sticking out of the rock face. Eventually, all the surrounding calcite was gone, and Peter's knob also fell down the cliff into a big rock pile. "I can't see much from here," he complained, hoping this situation would not last very long. Soon, the chert knob started to move. It was the beginning of a long journey. Peter was excited. His data showed that every once in a while, his chert knob moved a bit: sliding, gliding, jumping, and hopping. Sometimes it moved a centimeter. Other times, several meters. Eventually, he ended up in a riverbed. "Rivers—that's the way to travel efficiently," Peter learned. All the travel broke the chert knob into smaller pieces and rounded off the edges. This is how Peter changed. The chert knob didn't exist anymore. He became Peter Pebble.

Peter loved being a pebble. "I found my true destiny," he told the other pebbles in the riverbed. "I am not only at earth's surface and am able to collect data, I travel from one interesting place to another." This lifestyle came with a price though. Peter's constant movement often made him very dizzy. Sometimes he landed on his face, his right side, the left side, or upside-down. Peter did not complain. "Nothing is perfect." The river carried Peter out of the Rocky Mountains that had formed in the west and into the **foreland**. The river was now wide and had many arms that hugged elongated islands made of sand and gravel. Peter would sometimes hang out on one of these river islands before moving on again. Eventually, he found a good place and decided to stay. It was time to get some rest. "I need to think about all my observations and data," he thought happily. As he rested and reflected, more grains and pebbles arrived and buried him.

It was about 130 million years ago, in the Early Cretaceous time, when Peter lost sight of the sun. "I will be back," he muttered, still busy analyzing his data. There was a lot to think about. He slowly started to understand how earth works. He predicted he would be back and see the sun again.

Peter got buried by pebbles, sand, and mud that came from the growing Rocky Mountains in the west. Together with his new friends, Peter formed a pebbly neighborhood that transformed into a strong **conglomerate** rock layer. It did not take too long, and soon Peter heard a familiar noise. "I know what this is—the vibrating sound of breaking rocks." Peter was thrilled. "This is how mountain building feels. We will soon be uplifted and see the earth's surface again." Peter was right. Mountain building in the west had not ended, it had just taken a several-million-yearlong break. But now, in the Late Cretaceous times, a new generation of thrust faults emerged, rising from kilometer depths and breaking through rocks to get to the surface. These thrust heroes marched forcefully to the east, bulldozing over everything and stacking up rock layer over rock layer.

Although Peter was right about the thrusting, he was wrong about the uplift to the surface. When the shattering noise came really close, Peter's data showed that the load on top of him suddenly became much heavier. Peter panicked. He expected the thrust would ease the burden. He looked at his data. The temperature also showed that it got warmer, not colder. "We are suddenly much deeper below earth's surface than before," Peter realized.

It took about 20 million years before the shattering and quaking of the earth vanished in the east. Many more millions of years had to pass before Peter emerged at the surface. The carving power of **glaciers** finally moved the surrounding material away, slowly excavating the sturdy conglomerate of Peter's neighborhood. "At least I was right about the surface," Peter thought, relieved when he finally saw the sun again. That was a couple tens of thousands of years ago. He remembers how surprised he was when he saw how much earth's surface had changed.

The landscape was barren, rocks and ice everywhere. It took another while before the valley and the mountain slopes turned green. The trees and the animals he recorded were all different. No dinosaurs! Instead, there were sheep, bears, and marmots.

Today, Peter looks up to the peaks west of him. He is still fascinated by how the mountain building fooled him. "I had it so wrong." He smirks. He looks up to Mr. Rundle Thrust fault who sits just a bit above him. "He looks so peaceful now," Peter thinks, "but I know he can be a beast." When Mr. Rundle tried to emerge at the surface, he sliced through Peter's rock layer from below and placed the old Devonian limestone layers from deep below the surface on top of Peter's conglomerate. "I remember you guys," Peter thinks quietly while looking up to the steep rocky cliff above Mr. Rundle Thrust. "My childhood neighborhood was only a bit younger than you. I was born in the muddy deposits on top of you!" Peter chuckles. "But you old Devonian limestones have never been at the surface before." Happily, he keeps documenting his surroundings. His data shows he will be traveling again. He knows he will get buried again and, many million years later, exposed to the surface. "I wonder how earth's surface will look then," Peter thinks excitedly. "In any case, it will be worth documenting."

# SCIENCE FACTS

*Calcite* – A mineral that is also called calcium carbonate, $CaCO_3$. It is a very common mineral and occurs in a large variety of forms. Calcium carbonate rocks are also called limestone, marble, and chalk.

*Chert* – A very hard rock composed of micrometer-small crystals of quartz. Chert often occurs as thin and very hard layers within carbonate rocks.

*Conglomerate* – A sedimentary rock type composed of many pebbles and rock pieces that are held together by fine-grained sandy and muddy material.

**Craton** – Large landmasses of very old rocks, older than one billion years. Most of Canada is underlain by old craton rocks. Cratons can also be found in Australia, Brazil, southern Africa, and Greenland.

**Diagenetic** – The process of transforming loose and soft sediment (grains deposited in a seabed or riverbed) into a solid rock by burial with more sediment is called diagenesis. The deep burial causes pressures and temperatures to rise that squeeze out the water and bake the grains together.

**Fault** – A surface that splits a rock and moves one side in a different direction than the other side of the rock. Looking at a rock cliff, a fault usually looks like a line separating the two rock units. Faults can vary in size depending on how much they move and how long they move for.

**Foreland** – The region in front of the mountains where the sediment that is eroded from the mountains is deposited. Over millions of years, the mountains grow bigger and wider, and the foreland sediments are built into the mountains. At the same time, new foreland forms in front of the mountains.

**Glacier** – A mass of ice that forms at the high mountain peaks where it is cold and snowy. Like rivers, glaciers flow down the valley, but at a much slower pace. The Rocky Mountains were covered by glaciers over the past 2.6 million years. During that time, glaciers went through several cycles of growing and retreating as the climate shifted to colder and warmer times.

**Limestone** – A sedimentary rock type that is mostly composed of calcium carbonate $CaCO_3$. Limestone is often called carbonate rocks.

**Silica** – The dioxide form of silicon, $SiO_2$, also known as quartz. It is the most common mineral and occurs in many forms and has many names such as quartz, flint, or chert.

**Thrust** – One of the three types of faults and the most common type you can see in the Rocky Mountains. Old rocks from deep below earth's surface are thrusted on top of younger rocks at shallower depths.

# BRIDGET CEMENT
The hoodoos near Banff overlooking Bow River

Location: Hoodoo Lookout at
Tunnel Mountain Road, Banff

51.121117°N, 115.086667°

**B**ridget tightly hugs the grains around her. Keeping the grains together, that's her goal. It always has been. This effort has resulted in the beautiful **hoodoos** she is part of today. They are so different than the other rock formations around. While Bridget is proud to be part of these mysterious-looking hoodoos, she now sometimes questions her purpose. Looking down to the Bow River, the slope is so steep she almost gets dizzy. "Will I be strong enough?" she wonders. "One day, my hug may not be firm enough to hold all the grains together." The wind, the rain, and gravity all work against her. This is the daily battle Bridget fights today.

Back in the Pleistocene times, Bridget was born when it was very cold in Banff. It was during one of the last ice ages when a huge **glacier** crept down the Bow Valley. That was about 26 thousand years ago. The ice was hundreds of meters thick and scratched along the sides of the valley. These were rocky times! There were no trees or flowers, only ice, rocks, and dirt. Just the highest mountain peaks stuck out of the ice. From up in the sky, they watched the glacier flow while feeling the rocks being ripped out from beneath them. Like a bulldozer, the glacier moved boulders, rocks pieces, and lots of fine dirt down the valley. Bridget was born in such a pile of glacier **sediment** below the ice in Banff. Then the whole region became even messier once it got warmer and the ice started to melt. It began to thaw on all sides, leaving random blocks of ice and rocky piles of dirt in the valley. Water was everywhere. Lakes formed between ice blocks and dirt piles, and these lakes filled up with more rocky dirt that the rivers carried along.

The glacier sediment was very muddy and looked rather nasty from all the melting water around and atop. The water itself was loaded with **calcium** dissolved from the **limestone** rocks up the valley. This calcium was ready for action, forming new bonds and **crystallizing** into **calcite**. It was just a question of finding the right moment. Eventually, rivers started to run over the new glacial sediment layer, carving into the soft dirt. Action was needed now; waiting any longer would mean none of this rocky dirt would be preserved. This was the right time for the calcium to crystallize to calcite, forming Bridget **Cement**. Together with millions of her family members, they cemented the dirty mud—forming a rocky layer.

Because this all happened in a rush, the calcite crystals had no time to grow. Bridget was very tiny. She looked like a little speck sticking on larger grains. But she was strong and wanted to save the rocky dirt from being washed away. "I am going to cement you together," she said to the three grains that surrounded her. "This will make us stronger, almost like a rock." The grains did not say much but agreed to give Bridget and her cement family a chance to help them. This is how the loose, rocky dirt changed into a layer of hard, dirty rock. This all happened within only a couple of hundred years.

The glaciers came and went a couple more times, but overall, the climate got warmer and the glaciers smaller and smaller. The Bow Valley turned green. Trees and animals moved into the valley and the Bow River carved deep into the dirty rock layers left by the glaciers. The Bow River is Bridget's biggest enemy. It's not only constantly carving out the weakest rocks in the valley, but it also has the power to dissolve her. "Eventually, we will all end up in the river and we'll be carried who knows where!" she often worries. Sitting at the edge of a hoodoo, she has a good view of the river.

Today, Bridget looks over to the peaks behind Banff. She judges the clouds in the sky. "They look like nice-weather clouds," Bridget informs her neighborhood. "Looks like this will be an easy day for me." She smiles and loosens her grip on the grains slightly. Not every day is so relaxing; Banff gets a lot of bad-weather days. These are the days when Bridget cannot relax. They are hard-working times for her and her family. And sometimes these days end dramatically.

One such day occurred about twenty years ago when the winds blasted through the valley and at the hoodoos. "I can take the wind," Bridget shouted to her three grains, hugging them firmly. "But the blasting sand grains are brutal." These wind-blown grains pounded at the hoodoos. Suddenly, one of those grains hit Bridget and one of her grains really hard, knocking off their grip. "Oh no!" Bridget screamed over the loud wind when she lost her grain. Everything happened so fast; she couldn't even see the grain anymore. "I am so sorry," she sobbed, feeling that she had failed. "I hope the grain will be fine," she quietly thought. "But I am not failing you," she promised her other two grains, hugging them even more firmly than before. "I will protect you." Eventually, the wind calmed down and Bridget calmed too.

Bridget is thrilled to still be up here at the hoodoo pillars. Although she has endured many storms, she worries how many more they will survive. "After all, we are not as strong as the real rocks," she thinks while looking across the river to the rocky cliff on Mount Rundle. "Even these rocks **erode** and get carried away eventually. It just takes more time for them." Bridget is young, but she is a good observer. She has been around long enough to know how the valley and the mountains work. She knows that her glacial rock layer cannot compete with the old limestone rocks of the mountains. Those formed over hundreds of millions of years ago and were toughened by the kilometers of rocks that were laid on top of them. Bridget had heard the stories of these old rocks—the stories of Charles **Zircon,** Bob **Quartz,** and Lucy Calcite. The mountain building and all those things happened long before her.

Looking down to the Bow River, Bridget realizes how lazy the river is. "Always carving its paths in the weakest rock layers." She realizes that the river is smart. Why should it work harder if there is an easy way to carve a valley? "Maybe I should be more like the river?" Bridget ponders. "Is it necessary that I hug these grains so firmly?" Bridget suddenly questions her goal. She wonders if the time of cementing grains together is over. "Maybe the Bow River is not my enemy," she thinks, realizing that without the carving river, she would not be part of the hoodoos. The river and many storms made these landforms happen. For now, Bridget decides to keep hugging her grains, maybe a little less firmly. Soon, they will all end up in the river and get carried away. "Who knows where my help will be needed next," she thinks happily.

# SCIENCE FACTS

*Calcite* – A mineral also called calcium carbonate, $CaCO_3$. Calcite can form in the small spaces between sand grains and pebbles. This calcite is called cement, because it glues the grains together and transforms a loose pile of grains into a rock.

*Calcium* – A chemical element with the formula Ca. Calcium is built into many minerals such as calcite ($CaCO_3$), which composes most of the rocks in the Rocky Mountains. Calcite is easily dissolved in water and can be transported away. Similarly, calcium easily bonds with other atoms to form minerals such as calcite.

*Cement* – Any form of minerals that form between grains or rock pieces and glue them together. The process is called cementation and transforms loose material into a rock.

*Crystallizing* – The process of forming minerals by bonding together atoms in a specific order is called crystallization.

*Erode* – The process of removing rock from earth's surface is called erosion. There are many forces that cause erosion such as the power of glaciers, rivers, ocean waves, or strong winds.

*Glacier* – A mass of ice that forms at the high mountain peaks where it is cold and snowy. Like rivers, glaciers flow down the valley, but at a much slower pace. The Rocky Mountains were covered by glaciers over the past 2.6 million years. During that time, glaciers went through several cycles of advancing and retreating. You can see many leftover landforms in the Bow Valley that are the result of glaciation, including the hoodoos.

*Hoodoos* – Rocks that occur in the shape of thin, tall chimneys. Hoodoos are a landform and not a rock type. They form mostly in sedimentary rock layers that are soft and erode easily. A big boulder or pebble on top may protect the softer rock underneath from erosion. Like an umbrella, the strong rock shelters the weaker material underneath from being taken away by erosion. This protection leads to the chimney-like shapes. There are many hoodoos of glacial material in the Bow Valley. Hoodoos are also found in the prairies, such as in Drumheller. These rocks are much older (Cretaceous) in comparison to the glacier sediment near Banff.

**Limestone** – A sedimentary rock composed mostly of calcite minerals ($CaCO_3$). Limestone is also called carbonate rock. Most of the big cliff-forming peaks in the Rocky Mountains are made of limestone.

**Quartz** – A mineral composed of silica oxide $SiO_2$. Quartz is a very common mineral and forms large portions of rocks like granite, sandstones, or quartzite.

**Sediment** – Material that is transported by wind, water, or glaciers and deposited in layers in low-lying areas. Sediment transported by glaciers can be found in front and on the sides of the glacier (called moraines) but also underneath the glacier (called subglacial till). The sediment layer that forms the Banff hoodoos is believed to have formed as subglacial till. Because it was never buried deep, these sediments are very soft and are not real rock.

**Zircon** – A mineral with the formula $ZrSiO_4$ that is very hard and durable. Many rocks contain zircon, but only in very small amounts.

# RAY CLAY
Shale layer that separates the
cliffs of Castle Mountain

*Location: Castle Mountain
at Castle Junction*

*51.268402°N, 115.918629°W*

Ray looks over the Bow Valley from the lofty heights of Castle Mountain. Ray is not part of the steep rock cliff; he lives in the thin **shale** rock layer that separates the lower and upper **limestone** cliffs. Ray is a real genius—a mastermind with simple but brilliant ideas. But he is also rather shy by nature. Standing out from the crowd is not really his style. He much prefers to stay in the background. However, his brilliant ideas are what he wants recognized. Here at Castle Mountain, it is perfect as Ray is safely tucked away from the cliff edge. By doing so, he and his friends in the shale layer give the mountain its magnificent two-level look. Like a real castle.

Throughout his lifespan, Ray has had many brilliant ideas, but there is one he is most proud of, a task he started 505 million years ago and continues today: the perfect preservation of the first large animals that ever existed on earth. His secret animal archive is perfectly intact and teaches about the very deep past. However, despite all his diligent work and brilliant ideas, Ray and his shale community are often overlooked. They rarely get the recognition they deserve. Most of the attention is taken by the hundreds-of-meters-thick limestone layers. They stick out bold and steep, forming the castle's walls.

"They are so much braver than me," Ray thinks, admiring the confidence of the limestones. "I wish I could be a bit more like them." Ray never gets tired of looking at the impressive limestone peaks all around. They are the ones that give the Rocky Mountains their breathtaking look. "I always wanted my ideas to be useful and recognized by the world," Raymond mutters, wondering how the world is judging others. "But I know I'm useful and smart, even if I am not as flashy."

Ray was born over a billion years ago in the Proterozoic times, probably in what is now Manitoba or Saskatchewan. He does not remember the details. Who cares anyway? What he remembers is that he was born in a **magma** chamber together with many other shiny **minerals**. It was warm, squishy, and dark. Over millions of years, the magma chamber cooled into hard rocks and started to rise to the surface. Eventually, Ray and his neighboring minerals were exposed to the surface where they quickly **weathered** and were washed away by the rain. This was a painful time for Ray. The long travels on earth's surface knocked off several edges and pieces, changing Ray's look and size. His mineral structure and chemistry changed. The water leached out some of his elements and replaced them with others. Overall, Ray was in bad shape by the time he arrived at the ancient ocean that had formed in the west. "Finally, the ocean! I think this is the end of our journey," Ray said hopefully to his mineral friends. But not quite!

When Ray reached the ancient ocean beach, he was not only small, but also very light—a little shiny mineral flake. Unlike the other mineral grains that decided to settle here at the beach, he was too lightweight. The next ocean wave gently picked him up and took him away. That was in the Cambrian time when Alberta was near the equator. There were no palm trees and no plants or animals on land at all. The ocean water was tropical though. "Not a bad place for swimming!" Ray thought and continued his journey far out into the ocean. Ray was happy, feeling relaxed and accepted as part of the ocean. "Maybe I was not born to be part of a rock," he thought, "but rather a part of the ocean." There were so many others living in the ocean water, trillions of organisms, many of them with tiny shells and skeletons. They were all small like Ray. After a while, he realized he was sinking.

Slowly, he descended deep into the dark ocean. There were none of the small organisms around here. Eventually, Ray **Clay** settled on the deep ocean floor about 505 million years ago. "Wait a minute—what is that?" Ray was shocked at the enormously large and strange creature that lived on the ocean floor. Ray was fascinated by Tim **Trilobite**, who slowly crawled closer. "Earth is amazing! They now have life that is much bigger than a mineral grain. This guy is gigantic! At least a couple centimeters long." Ray was a little scared, wondering if the trilobite would harm him. But at the same time, Ray was eager to learn more about Tim and his family members. Their shape was so complex. There was a head, body, legs, and an internal motor that moved all these parts. As Tim moved closer, Ray whispered, "This is the coolest thing I have ever seen. There is life—complex life—here in the darkness of the deep ocean floor!"

Over the next couple years, Ray became more and more familiar with Tim and the other trilobites. The trilobites were a real hit! The superstars of their time. They came in a large variety of shapes and sizes. Some of them had a skeleton they wore on the outside of their body like a shield. Tim and the other trilobites walked right over the soft clays with their many legs, only tickling and squeezing Ray. He was grateful for the trilobites. The dark ocean floor would be rather dull without them. Tim and his trilobite friends were very entertaining and got all the attention, which allowed Ray to study them carefully.

However, it did not take long for Ray to discover that the trilobites were not perfect. They had one major flaw—they did not live forever. Like all organisms, the trilobites appeared very energetic after they were born, but as they grew older, their energy decreased. They all died after a short while and their dead bodies lay around on the seabed. This is where Ray had his brilliant idea. "Future generations need to know about the trilobites," he decided, "and we can preserve them." Turning to his clay friends, he explained, "We can make a perfect cast of their entire bodies. We can preserve their skeleton and their flesh, legs, and head." Because Ray and the clay minerals were so small and soft, they could lie around each little corner and wrinkle of the trilobite body. This is how Ray, together with millions of other clay minerals, made a perfect cast of Tim.

Over the next millions of years, very slowly, more clays settled on top of Ray, Tim, and the other trilobites, building up a layer of dark, muddy shale. Sometime later, the water level of the ancient ocean changed dramatically, bringing the ocean floor into much shallower waters. This allowed the rapid growth of thick layers of **carbonates**, like the one where Lucy **Calcite** lives.

The times of depositing more and more **sediment** layers on the ancient ocean floor lasted very long, about 300 million years or so. With every layer deposited, the pressure and heat increased, becoming unbearable for Ray. Once again, these new conditions forced him to change. The heavy load of the overlying, younger rock layers pressed Ray and Tim even closer together. This is when Ray's muddy layer of clays turned into a layer of shale rock.

"We are not one of the strong rocks, but we are rocks for sure." Ray is still proud to have survived the heat and pressure that turned them into a rock community. "We even survived the times of mountain building that was going on a little while ago." Ray vividly remembers the rumbling **earthquake** thunders caused by the breaking of large rock layers that slid on top of each other. He heard the painful stories of rocks that were affected badly, but mountain building did not bother Ray too much. The thick and strong carbonate layers above and below Ray protected him. Sandwiched between these much stronger rocks, Ray's shale community was only lifted up and pushed east a couple kilometers. That all happened early in the makings of the Rocky Mountains, around 160 million years ago in the Late Jurassic times. The earth shaking lasted for another hundred million years, but it was mostly in the distance and appeared to move farther to the east.

"It's sometimes good to have strong neighbors." Ray looks at the limestone cliff above and below them. "I would not be here without their protection. And I would certainly not be high up on a peak with such a great view." Ray knows that most shale rock layers crumble up into gentle slopes that are covered by trees.

Ray is mostly proud of his shale community today. There are new critters these days—humans—that walk all over him. They are searching for Tim and the other trilobite **fossils**. "I was right—the future generations are interested to learn about Tim and his life 505 million years ago." He knows that other rock layers have tried to preserve organisms too, but none have done such a brilliant job of preserving the very fine details. "We clays did a truly expert job," he thinks. He is proud of his diligent work helping others learn about the past.

# SCIENCE FACTS

*Calcite* – A mineral, also called calcite carbonate, with the chemical formula of $CaCO_3$. Most calcite carbonate forms thick sediment layers in ocean basins, particularly when the ocean water is warm and not very deep. Some rocks are composed entirely of calcite minerals and are called carbonates or limestone.

*Carbonate* – A rock type composed of carbonate minerals such as calcite or dolomite. Most of the big cliff-forming rock layers you can see in the Rocky Mountains are carbonates.

*Clay* – A mineral group that is composed of silica layers with a large variety of elements that are built in between the layers. With changing temperatures, pressures, and chemistry, clay minerals change easily from one kind to another, and can also change their size.

*Earthquake*– The shaking of earth when rocks break on a large scale. During Rocky Mountain building, the rock layers were pushed together from the side, which caused breaking of rock layers and forming of large faults. The breaking process itself creates an intense shaking of the rocks deep below earth surface. This shaking is what we call earthquake.

*Fossil* – A rock record of an ancient organism in the form of an imprint, bones, shells, footprints, or others. Fossils can teach us about the evolution of life over geologic times. They can also tell us about the environment in the past where the organism lived in. For example, if they lived in the deep oceans or shallow waters on the shore.

*Limestone* – A sedimentary rock composed mostly of calcite minerals ($CaCO_3$). Limestone is also called carbonate rock.

*Magma* – A mixture of liquid rock material, solid mineral crystals, and gas bubbles. Magma occurs in kilometer-big magma chambers, large bodies of hot and soft rock material located several kilometers below the surface. Many minerals are formed and grow in magma chambers due to slow cooling, a process called crystallization.

**Mineral** – The building blocks of rocks. Minerals are composed of various chemical elements that build specific crystal structures. Minerals vary in their grain size from a few micrometers to millimeters; only sometimes do they grow to centimeter sizes.

**Sediment** – Loose material that is transported by wind, water, or glaciers and deposited in horizontal layers in low- lying areas. Most sediment comes from mountains and is transported into oceans. The process of sedimentation continuous for millions of years, building up kilometers of thick layers of sediment in oceans. The deep burial of sediment transforms it into sedimentary rocks.

**Shale** – A sedimentary rock that is composed mostly of clays and other mineral grains that are very small. The grain size is called clay-size and is similar to flour. You cannot feel the grains when rubbing them between your fingers.

**Trilobite** – A large group of animals that lived in ancient oceans from about 520 to 250 million years ago. Many of the trilobites had an external skeleton. The Burgess shale located near Field (Yoho National Park) is a famous location for fossil trilobites. The Burgess shale was deposited at the same time as the shale at Castle Mountain. The layer of the shale is just thinner at Castle Mountain in comparison to farther west.

**Weathered** – The processes of breaking down or dissolving rocks and mineral is called weathering. There are many weathering processes such as freezing and thawing of water that open cracks in the rock until they become very large. Chemical weathering can dissolve specific mineral or replace atoms within a mineral, forming a new one.

# ABOUT THE AUTHOR

Eva Enkelmann is a geology professor at the University of Calgary and researches mountain-building processes and educates the next generations of scientists. She is an elected fellow of the Geological Society of America and has published more than seventy peer-reviewed papers in international journals.

As a geologist, she is trained to listen to the rocks, read their minds, and uncover their stories from over hundreds of millions of years. She loves the outdoors and spends most of her free time climbing, hiking, and skiing in the Rocky Mountains. She also loves to take her students into the mountains for field trips.

She was born and raised in Germany and worked in the US for ten years before she came to Calgary, Alberta, in 2017.

Her website is: www.enkelmann.org
You can follow her on Twitter: @GeoEnkelmann

CPSIA information can be obtained
at www.ICGtesting.com
Printed in the USA
LVHW071552190323
741963LV00009B/325

9 781039 161542